Accession no.
00939897

D1744851

Studies in International Economics and Institutions

Editor
Hans-Jürgen Vosgerau

Advisory Board
John S. Chipman
Elhanan Helpman
Ronald W. Jones
Murray C. Kemp
Horst Siebert

Studies in International Economics and Institutions

H.-J. Vosgerau (Ed.), New Institutional Arrangements for the World Economy
IX, 482 pages. 1989

M. Rauscher, OPEC and the Price of Petroleum
XII, 206 pages. 1989

F. Gehrels, H. Herberg, H. Schneider, H.-J. Vosgerau (Eds.), Real Adjustment Processes under Floating Exchange Rates
VI, 302 pages, 1990

T. Tivig, Flexible Wechselkurse aus der Sicht des Finanzmarktansatzes
IX, 226 Seiten, 1991

Siegfried Berninghaus
Hans Günther Seifert-Vogt

International Migration Under Incomplete Information

A Microeconomic Approach

With 16 Figures

CHESTER COLLEGE
ACC. No. 00939897
DEPT.
CLASS No. 519.2024337 BER
LIBRARY

Springer-Verlag
Berlin Heidelberg New York London Paris
Tokyo Hong Kong Barcelona Budapest

Professor Dr. Siegfried Berninghaus
Universität Mannheim, Fakultät für Volkswirtschaftslehre und Statistik, A 5, D-6800 Mannheim 1, FRG

Dr. Hans Günther Seifert-Vogt
Gnadenseestraße 15a, D-7760 Radolfzell 18, FRG

ISBN 3-540-54091-1 Springer-Verlag Berlin Heidelberg New York Tokyo
ISBN 0-387-54091-1 Springer-Verlag New York Heidelberg Berlin Tokyo

This work is subject to copyright. All rights are reserved, whether the whole or part of the material is concerned, specifically the rights of translation, reprinting, reuse of illustration, recitation, broadcasting, reproduction on microfilms or in other ways, and storage in data banks. Duplication of this publication or parts thereof is only permitted under the provisions of the German Copyright Law of September 9, 1965, in its version of June 24, 1985, and a copyright fee must always be paid. Violations fall under the prosecution act of the German Copyright Law.

© Springer-Verlag Berlin · Heidelberg 1991
Printed in Germany

The use of registered names, trademarks, etc. in this publication does not imply, even in the absence of a specific statement, that such names are exempt from the relevant protective laws and regulations and therefore free for general use.

Printing: Weihert-Druck GmbH, Darmstadt
Bookbinding: J. Schäffer GmbH u. Co. KG., Grünstadt
2142/7130-543210

Preface

This research monograph comprises results that have been derived while both authors were working at the research project "International Migration under Incomplete Information" that has been integrated into the Sonderforschungsbereich "Internationalisierung der Wirtschaft", established in 1986 at the University of Konstanz. Financial support of the **Deutsche Forschungemeinschaft** is gratefully acknowledged. Most of our results have been discussed intensively with our colleagues in the stimulating atmosphere of the Sonderforschungsbereich and they have already been presented at several national and international meetings. Some of the results have been published in a modified form in diverse journals (for details see the list of references). It is our main aim in the present monograph to give a unified framework for our conclusions in the theory of migration. Furthermore, many recent results that have not been published yet are added. As we regard migration as an essentially dynamic phenomenon involving incompletely informed agents emphasis is laid in this monograph on the rigorous derivation of the characteristics of migration decision–making by applying recent results in the theory of Stochastic Dynamic Optimization. We know from other branches in economics that it may be dangerous to draw policy implications from an individual decision–making model. Therefore we take account of interactions between migrants' supply and demand in an equilibrium framework (see chapter III).

Work on international migration has been mostly empirical on an aggregate level in the past. That is why we were mainly interested in developing the microtheoretical aspects of international migration. However, we did not consider it reasonable to finish this monograph without any advice for the econometric modelling of the theoretical framework. Therefore we decided to insert a chapter on this subject (chapter IV). This chapter has a more expository character than the remaining ones. Nevertheless it seemed to be an appropriate supplement for the theoretical part of our monograph.

Finally we would like to mention three colleagues without whose support this monograph would not have been finished. We want to thank Professor John McCall who introduced us to the field of applications of the Gittins–index method. He encouraged us in many stimulating discussions and gave us valuable advice. We also want to thank Professor Hans Jürgen Ramser, director of the "migration" research project, who supervised progress in work on this monograph. Without his perpetual efforts the "migration" project would not have been established at all. In this context we also have to thank Professor Hans–Jürgen Vosgerau, the director of the Sonderforschungsbereich, who helped us in getting financial support and other necessary resources for terminating this monograph.

We are not able to thank all people by name who contributed to the monograph either by technical or by professional advice with the exception of the following three persons. We thank Monika Ruschinski and Wolfgang Ernst for carefully reading the manuscript. And finally we are deeply indebted to Barbara Lüthke who really did an excellent job in typing the manuscript. Anyone who only takes a glimpse at the appendix for example will recognize this.

Konstanz/Mannheim

November, 1990

Contents

Introduction

It is presumably undisputed among economists, social scientists and demographers that a key factor influencing the migration behaviour besides the pecuniary aspects is the 'quality of life'. Concerning the concept we intend to subsume all the factors that influence the subjective well–being of an individual, like the cultural climate, the education system, the acceptance by the neighbourhood, the working conditions etc. On the other hand it must be expected that a potential migrant especially in international migration will typically be informed only partially or at least rather vaguely about the pecuniary aspects and the quality of life in his prospective guest country before migration. Only by living there i. e. after migration, the individual will become well or at least better informed.

It seems to us that various stories can be told intending the generation of hypotheses concerning the influence of incomplete information about those factors on individual and aggregate migration behaviour. Depending on the theoretical and methodological background, each hypothesis seems to be more or less plausible. A look at the empirical studies of migratory movements shows that it is in general impossible to obtain definitive falsifications of these hypotheses exclusively by statistical methods. These "observations" motivated us to clarify the theoretical and methodological background on which our own hypotheses are based. This information constitutes an indispensable tool for the "users" of the results, if they are trying to judge the applicability of these results for answering questions of practical and/or theoretical interest.

For the clarification of this background we regard two ingredients as crucial:

i) the intended use of the envisaged model, and

ii) the paradigm which covers the view of the world.

Whereas the first ingredient may vary between different researchers of the same discipline, the second ingredient will typically be different for researchers of different disciplines.

With respect to i) our main concern will be – as outlined above – to describe the informational aspects of international (human) migration. In general we will be interested in the role of informational deficits about the pecuniary and non–pecuniary factors.

Our paradigm will be the traditional neoclassical view of decision–making: the individual migrant will be regarded as a utility maximizing agent. More specifically, confronted with uncertainty, a potential migrant is modelled as an agent who is gathering information and deciding between the options "migration" and "non–migration" according to rules which follow from a sophisticated expected utility maximizing approach. An important novelty of the approach in this monograph – compared with other work about incomplete information in the migratory context (see e. g. Molho (1986) for an overview) is the sequential decision–making framework which will be used. By this method we want to capture the undisputable stylized fact that the migration decision can at least partially be reversed or altered by remigration or repeated migration provided the circumstances at the first place of destination turn out to be unfavourable. In our opinion this possibility is so evident for a decision maker in a migration decision problem that it seems reasonable to highlight this fact in a theoretical model – and the best known approach to do this is the sequential decision–making framework.

Based on this background it will be the main purpose of our book to present the theoretical foundations for a sound empirical measurement of the effects of incomplete information on pecuniary and non–pecuniary factors in international migration. We are concentrating on international migration, since here the incomplete information aspect seems to be rather evident and since it seems highly desirable, that some progress in research on international migration has to be made, from a practical and a theoretical point of view.

The book will be organized as follows: In chapter I the sequential decision framework for individual migration decisions will be developed in rather general terms, emphasis beeing placed on the incomplete information aspect. In section I.3 an important specialization of the general model is discussed in full detail: the Multi–Armed–Bandit–model of international migration. It will be demonstrated that the method of Gittins–indices – first applied to the analysis of labour migration by McCall/McCall (1984)[1] – serves as a useful tool for describing migration decision behavior in the MAB–framework. Under specific assumptions, among others risk–neutrality of the migrant, some hypotheses interesting from an economic point of view will be derived. Section I.4 is devoted to a detailed discussion of the validity of these hypotheses in the case of risk-averse migrants.

In chapter II a rather urgent theme in the context of international (guest–worker) migration is taken up, the phenomenon of 'temporary vs. permanent' migration. As the "target–saver" point of view on guest–worker migration seems to be an appropriate paradigm for modelling temporary migration decision making, we use the general model of chapter I.2 supplemented by the explicit possibility of taking account of saving or consumption decisions. And we are able to provide an explanation of the 'temporary–vs.–permanent–migration'–phenomenon in decision theoretical terms.

Since observed migration behaviour during a larger time period will not only be the result of individual migration decisions but also of the opportunities the labour market offers to the individuals, and since it must be expected that these labour market conditions are to a non–negligible extent determined by past–migration decisions, it seems natural to extend our partial–partial equilibrium framework of individual migration decision to a partial equilibrium model. This will be done in chapter III. Here we present a temporary equilibrium model of international migration with overlapping generations and incomplete information. The purpose of this model is to analyze whether the main implications of the

[1]This paper was the starting point of our work on the aspects of incomplete information in international migration. J. McCall's helpful suggestions are gratefully acknowledged.

partial–partial equilibrium framework remain valid in the more general set–up and further to yield some conclusions about aggregate migration behaviour in a dynamic context. We dispense with the construction of a general equilibrium model where the production factor capital would also be endogenously determined: in our approach capital is exogenously given, since we are not able at this point to present a theory of migration of physical capital.

Chapter IV is intended to illustrate how econometric modelling may be supported by our theoretical models. Principally this can be done in a twofold way: one way is to specify models which are designed for the use of individual micro–data about migrants and to try some discrete–choice analysis for the econometric measurement of the main parameters of the theoretical models (this approach will be exemplified by a model of remigration behaviour of guest–workers from a receiving country, e. g. West Germany, to a sending country, e. g. Turkey). The second way is to construe a model of aggregate migration behaviour, where still some of the parameters may be interpreted as those of the individual migration decisions, and then to use data about aggregate migration streams to measure these parameters (the second approach will be illustrated by an econometric model of guest–worker migrations to and from West–Germany). With respect to the above–mentioned econometric models it must be remarked that at the moment only parts of the enormous technical problems (like data collection, computation of the estimation procedures) could be regarded as satisfactorily solved. Thus we have not been able yet to present concrete numerical results – these will be published later elsewhere. But this does not seem to us to be a serious flaw. For the main purpose of the present volume is to give a consistent theoretical foundation for the analysis of the most relevant aspects of international migration under incomplete information, and to demonstrate how the key concepts of the theoretical model can be measured by econometric methods, at least principally.

Chapter I

Migration as a Sequential Decision Problem under Uncertainty

I.1 Introductory Remarks

The main subject of the present chapter is the presentation of a logically consistent model for individual migration decision-making. More precisely, we consider the problem of a potential migrant who has the opportunity to move into one of N countries, indexed by j for at least one period. It is natural to assume that the migrant is incompletely informed about the pecuniary and non-pecuniary variables in the countries in question. As the migrant might encounter unexpectedly unfavourable values of these variables, he might decide to leave the country he tried out for at least one period and either move back into his home country or move to a different country. That is, at each decision time point the migrant must be able to revise his decision in face of incoming information.

In the following sections, we will formulate precisely the meaning of "incomplete information" in different contexts and we will construe a general framework for sequential decision-making over a given planning horizon. In I.2 we introduce the central concepts of a Markovian decision process that will serve as a general framework for all the special decision models for migration used in this monograph. More precisely, a potential migrant is seen as a decision-maker in a Markov decision process. The **set of alternatives** is the set of countries where the migrant could migrate. At least principally he can decide more than once, such that the model allows room for repeated migration and especially for remigration. It is assumed that a migration decision is influenced by the **states of the countries**, which will typically be given as pecuniary and non-pecuniary factors (real wages and indices of qualities of life in the different countries), or as states of information about those factors; furthermore by the **migrant's preferences** of these states, by his time preference and last but not least by his information on how these states will evolve during the decision process. The idea that the migrant can gather information, that new information would eventually cause a revision of a previous migration decision, and that the migrant is able to foresee this ex-ante, is captured by the concept of a **stochastic law of motion** of the decision process. Migration behavior will then be described as the result of an optimal migration strategy in this process.

Section I.3. is devoted to the analysis of a concrete model of migration decision–making and the determination of the optimal migration policy. By some specializing assumptions the general Markovian decision process can be regarded as a **Multi–armed bandit problem**. For Multi–armed bandit problems of the kind we need in migration theory there is a powerful solution method, called **Gittins–index theory**, that will be utilized to derive optimal migration policies. Gittins–index theory can roughly be characterized as a method for determining the optimal sequence of pursuing a particular activity (taken from a finite set of activities) during specified time periods. Typically the state of each activity will change according to a stochastic law if the activity will be worked. As each state of an activity is furthermore associated with a (possibly monetary) payoff, the decision maker faces a sequential decision problem under uncertainty where he tries to control the selection of activities such that the expected total discounted payoff (over a specified planning horizon) will be made as large as possible. It was Gittins and his colleagues (e. g. Gittins/Jones (1974), Gittins/Nash (1974)) who demonstrated that the optimal policy for this complicated sequential decision problem can be described by a rather simple procedure: to each activity there is associated a real number (called "Gittins–index") which is dependent on the state of the activity. Then the decision maker has to choose at each decision point, the activity with the largest Gittins–index. Furthermore the Gittins–index can be given an interesting economic interpretation depending on the problem at hand. In recent years the range of potential applications has been broadened considerably by generalizing the Gittins–index method to a very general formal framework (see Varayia et al. (1984), Mandelbaum (1986)). In our model we use Gittins–index policy to describe the optimal migration policy of a potential migrant.

By applying this method it is possible to deal with most of the dynamic migration phenomena caused by incomplete information (as remigration, increased mobility after migration etc.) within a model of rational decision making. Clearly this is the main advantage of our model which can be regarded as a substantial improvement upon the "classical" Human Capital approach to migration[2] and its modifications (e. g. Sjaastad (1962), Cebula (1978), Todaro (1969)). In recent years there has been some work done which is similar to ours. G. Mayer (1985) applies the theory of Optimal Stopping in face of an unknown distribution (over wages) to the problem of migration under incomplete information. Mayer demonstrates that the migration policy can be described by a generalized reservation wage policy. In McCall/McCall (1987) the framework is extended such that there is supposed incomplete information not only about the economic variables in the foreign regions but also about non–monetary returns. Furthermore by applying Gittins–index theory McCall/McCall found an appropriate framework to deal with remigration. Our model can be regarded as a substantial generalization of McCall's model. We are able to demonstrate that one can abandon most of the restrictions concerning the information structure in McCall's paper.

Finally in section I.4 we analyze the effects of risk–aversion on the optimal migration behaviour. This particular analysis has been motivated by one of the main results of

[2]The literature on migration cited here is mainly concerned with **internal** migration. But the extension to **international** migration (which we have in mind here) is straightforward.

section I.3, where we will demonstrate that "more uncertainty"[3] in the probability distribution over the relevant variables in a country will raise the attractivity of this country for migration. This – at a first glance – paradoxical result is based, beside some other factors, on the risk–neutrality of the migrant. In I.4 we can demonstrate that the "paradoxical" result can be extended to the case of risk–averse migrants, provided they are not "too risk–averse". As it needs some technical elaboration to formulate precisely the term "too risk–averse" section I.4 is a little bit harder to read than the remaining sections from a technical point of view. It may be skipped at a first reading.

I.2 A General Formal Model of a Decision Process for International Migration

In the present section we will introduce a particular Markovian decision process that turns out to be an appropriate formal framework for decision–making in international migration. We will primarily discuss the crucial concepts of a Markovian decision process where main emphasis is laid on the interpretation of these concepts for migration decision–making rather than on technical questions like measurability, integrability etc. (for a more technical description see for example Berninghaus (1984)).

I.2.1 States and Actions

We suppose that the individual migrant has to make a decision at finitely many or countably infinite decision time points $t = 0, 1, 2, \ldots, T$ $(T \leq \infty)$. At each decision time point t the individual has to choose to move into one of N countries (indexed by j). Therefore the **action space** of the Markovian decision process is given by the finite set

$$A := \{1, \ldots, N\} \tag{1}$$

If the individual is living in country j in period $[t, t+1)$ he is confronted with the "state" $s_j(t)$ which can change from one period to another. The **state space** for the decision process is then given by the Cartesian product of the countries' states

$$S := S_1 \times \ldots \times S_N, \tag{2}$$

where each country's state space S_j is supposed to be a subset of some finite or infinite dimensional vector space depending on the economic interpretation of a "state of a country".

Before giving some concrete specifications for the state spaces we can briefly characterize the structure of the Markovian decision process as we will need it for the following. Given a state $s(t) \in S$ at decision time point t, that is a description of the states of all countries, the individual migrant will take an action in A. Then the whole state vector

[3] Uncertainty (resp. risk) in a probability distribution will be measured by the "mean preserving spread" of the distribution.

$s(t)$ might change from one period to the other according to a stochastic transition law. And the individual has to choose again an action in the following period taking account of the new state[4] $s(t+1)$.

Before proceeding with further concepts in the theory of Markovian decision processes we want to give two economic interpretations of the states $s_j(t)$ that will be utilized throughout the book.

I.2.1.1 "States of the Economy"–Interpretation

Here a state of a country in period $[t, t+1)$ will be interpreted as the realized values of selected economic variables in this country that are supposed to be crucial for the migration decision. According to the particular aspect of the migration problem these variables can be the real wage rates prevailing in country j during period $[t, t+1)$, denoted by $w_j(t)$, and the quality of life in country j, denoted by $x_j(t)$. Under the quality of life we will subsume all factors that may influence the subjective well-being of the individual migrant as the cultural climate, the educational system, the acceptance by the neighbourhood etc. For the sake of simplicity we assume that the quality of life can be represented by a real number expressing its monetary equivalent that can be added to the wage rate. In this sense, quality of life experience works like a correction of the wage rate. The state of country j may then be represented by the vector

$$s_j(t) = (w_j(t), x_j(t)) \in \mathbf{R}^2, \tag{3}$$

and consequently the state space S is supposed to be a particular subset of the $\mathbf{R}^{2N}$.

In focusing on the consumption and saving aspect of the migration decision we need a modified concept of state of an economy. Here we will interprete the state of a country as a vector of income y, prices p and wealth v, that is

$$s_j(t) = (p_j(t), y_j(t), v_j(t)) \in \mathbf{R}^3, \tag{4}$$

where we consider only one–dimensional price systems $p_j(t)$, that could better be interpreted as a price index for country j prevailing during period $[t, t+1)$. And $y_j(t)$ denotes the real income the migrant can earn in period $[t, t+1)$ in country j.

According to our brief remarks about Markovian decision processes, decision–making will take place at the particular decision time points after states have changed. Therefore our state space interpretation given above makes sense in a long–run framework, where a period takes several years. In this case one can assume that the economic conditions in each country, that is the states $s_j(t)$, may change from one period to another.

I.2.1.2 "States of Information"–Interpretation

In contrast to the previous interpretation, a state of country j prevailing during period $[t, t+1)$ is here regarded as a state of information about the values of the relevant economic

[4] Here it is implicitly assumed that the decision maker does not take care of the whole history of states and actions that have realized in the meantime. In the literature on Markovian decision processes rigorous conditions are given that justify this behaviour.

variables in country j. There is underlying the assumption that the values of the economic variables remain fixed throughout the decision process but unknown to the decision maker. Consequently this interpretation seems to make sense preferably for "short–run" decision problems, where the values of the economic variables do not change significantly. A state $s \in S$ is then interpreted as the decision maker's information about all countries. And a change in states from one period to another is interpreted as a change of information of the decision maker. In the following we will assume that no information gets lost during the migration decision process.

Obviously there is no unique way of formalizing the concept of state of information. We will present two different ways below. Primarily let us consider a migrant who is supposed to be incompletely informed about wages and the quality of life in a country. Then we will sometimes utilize the following schematical sequence of information acquisition about country j: the decision process starts with the artificial state

$$s_{0j} \quad \ldots \quad \text{"no information about country } j\text{"},$$

if the migrant moves to country j for one period the state of information will change to $s_j(1) = w_j$. That is, the migrant is supposed to be completely informed about the wage he can earn in country j after one period of living there. This corresponds to the result of the migrant's job search process in country j. Here we consider a given wage dispersion in country j that will not change during the decision process. Usually the migrant will not be completely informed about all wage opportunities at the end of his search process.

After one further period of living in country j the migrant is supposed to be completely informed about the quality of life in country j. In other words, the state of information changes to $s_j(2) = (w_j, x_j)$. As the migrant is now supposed to be completely informed about the relevant variables in country j the state of information will not change any more. Technically speaking, the decision maker has reached an absorbing state. The state space for country j can then be regarded as a subset[5]

$$S_j \subset \{s_{0j}\} \cup \mathbf{R}_+ \cup (\mathbf{R}_+ \times \mathbf{R}). \tag{5}$$

In a simplified version of this information gathering problem we sometimes suppose that the migrant is already completely informed about the wage rate he can earn in country j before he moves to this country. This assumption seems to make sense for example for guestworker migration, where labour contracts are fixed before moving into the country. In this case there is only incomplete information about the quality of life in country j. Consequently the state space can be regarded as a subset

$$S_j \subset \{s_{0j}\} \cup \mathbf{R}, \tag{6}$$

where we make the same assumptions about the process of information gathering as before.

Naturally this is a highly stylized picture of migrants real world information gathering processes. On the other hand it seems to be a fruitful simplification of the real world situation that is manageable in a formal decision model. Additionally we do not believe

[5]We suppose that the quality of life x_j might be any real number, that is $x_j \in \mathbf{R}$.

that more sophisticated information gathering procedures of the traditional approach to the state will change our results considerably.

For the sake of completeness we briefly mention a more traditional approach to the state of information concept that we will not utilize any further in this monograph. This approach accords with the Bayesian point of view. Here a state of information $s_j(t)$ about (w_j, x_j) may be defined as a probability measure over the set $(\mathbf{R}_+ \times \mathbf{R})$. In this case the state space for a country s_j would be regarded as a subset of the set of all probability measures over $(\mathbf{R}_+ \times \mathbf{R})$, denoted by $M(\mathbf{R}_+ \times \mathbf{R})$. That is, we have

$$S_j \subset M(\mathbf{R}_+ \times \mathbf{R}). \tag{7}$$

Then a change of state from $s_j(t)$ to $s_j(t+1)$ is controlled by the experience the migrant makes during the period and may be formalized by Bayesian adaptation of probability measures.

I.2.2 State Transitions

As already mentioned before, the states of all countries may change from one period to another stochastically. It is characteristic for a Markovian decision process that the stochastic state transition depends on the previous state and the action the decision maker took previously. More precisely, the **stochastic law of motion** is given generally by a sequence of transition probabilities $\{P_t(\cdot|\cdot)\}_{t=0}^T$, where $P_t(B|s,a)$ denotes the probability that the state will be in[6] $B(\in B(S))$ at time t, provided the system was in state s during period $[t-1,t)$ and action a has been taken during this period. It is easy to see that by the sequence of transition probabilities there is induced a Markov process of states on the space $\bigotimes_{t=0}^T S$ that is "controlled" in the given sense by the decision makers' actions. In our applications we will mostly deal with homogeneous Markov processes. Consequently we can omit the time index and talk about the transition law $P(\cdot|\cdot)$.

This state transition law is introduced for the "complete states" of all countries

$$s = (s_1, \ldots, s_N) \in \bigotimes_{j=1}^N S_j$$

of the decision problem. Concerning the "state of information"–interpretation of the states $s_j \in S_j$ it seems sometimes plausible to assume that only the state of information about one country changes from one period to the other. In this case only the j–th component of a state s would change from one period to another. It is easy to see that this special state transition can also be formalized within our general framework.

The state transition law will mostly be based on subjective probability estimation of a potential migrant. Let us consider for example the "state of the economy"–interpretation, where $s_j(t)$ denotes the wage rate and the quality of life $(w_j(t), x_j(t))$ in country j prevailing in period $[t, t+1)$. Then the transition probability can be interpreted as the subjective

[6]Here we denote by $B(S)$ the σ–algebra of all Borel subsets of S

probability of an individual migrant for the expected economic states prevailing in the following period.

The particular migration decision models introduced below mainly differ from each other with respect to the definition of $P(\cdot|\cdot)$. Therefore we will give the precise definitions where they are needed in the text.

I.2.3 Reward Function

To complete the description of a migrant's decision process we have to introduce an economic criterion by which it is possible to evaluate the states of the decision process. For this sake we specify per period utility functions $\{u_j(\cdot)\}_{j=1}^{N}$, where

$$u_j : s_j \rightarrow \mathbf{R} \tag{8}$$

represents the migrant's individual preferences about the possible states $s_j(t)$ in country j. This specification may be justified by the argument that the migrant may feel differently in different countries.

Corresponding to the state interpretations above we have also different interpretations of the utility functions: for the "state of the economy" interpretation we regard $u_j(w_j, x_j)$ and $u_j(p_j, y_j)$ respectively as the indirect utility the migrant can extract from wages, prices etc. in country j. Sometimes it is useful to work with additively separable, linear utility functions. In this case we would have, for example

$$u_j(w_j, x_j) = w_j + x_j. \tag{9}$$

Concerning the "state of information" interpretation the following definition of $u_j(\cdot)$ turns out to be useful later on. Primarily we consider the special case where the migrant has to pursue a job search process before:

$$\begin{aligned} u_j(s_{0j}) &:= -c_j, \\ u_j(s_j(1)) &:= (w_j - k_j) \qquad (s_j(1) = w_j), \\ u_j(s_j(2)) &:= (w_j + v_j(x_j)) \qquad (s_j(2) = (w_j, x_j)), \end{aligned} \tag{10}$$

where c_j denotes the search costs[7] for finding the optimal job offer in country j, and k_j denotes the migration costs of moving into country j. Finally $v_j(\cdot)$ is a utility function over non–pecuniary factors (= quality of life) in country j. Sometimes $v_j(\cdot)$ is supposed to be linear, which would imply the same representation as in (9).

If we consider the special case, where the migrant is already completely informed about the wage he can earn in country j, then the job–search phase can be omitted and the interpretation of the per period utility functions is given as follows:

$$\begin{aligned} u_j(s_{0j}) &:= (w_j - k_j), \\ u_j(s_j(1)) &:= (w_j + v_j(x_j)). \end{aligned} \tag{10'}$$

[7] We do not model this search process explicitly. Therefore c_j cannot be interpreted as the search costs per search step, but rather as the average costs for the total search process.

Concerning the migration costs k_j we intend a rather broad interpretation as it is usual in the theory of migration (see e. g. Greenwood (1975)). That is, we subsume not only transportation costs and other out of pocket costs under k_j, but also the opportunity costs of becoming familiar with the environment in the foreign country and furthermore the so–called "psychic costs" of migration. The latter costs arise from leaving friends and relatives and the familiar environment in the home country. Concerning this interpretation of migration costs there are serious measurement problems. But we will not deal with these problems in the theoretical part of the present monograph, where the results mostly are independent of the particular interpretation of the concepts.

If we consider the "state of information"–interpretation, where a state $s_j(t)$ is defined as a probability distribution over (w_j, x_j) a natural candidate for the per period utility function $u_j(\cdot)$ over the states would be the expected utility

$$u_j\left(s_j(t)\right) := \int_{\mathbf{R}_+ \times \mathbf{R}} \tilde{u}(w_j, x_j) ds_j(t), \tag{11}$$

where $\tilde{u}(\cdot)$ denotes the indirect utility function over wages and quality of life.

From these per period utility functions we can construe the **reward function** $u(\cdot)$ of the Markovian decision process with

$$u : S \times A \to \mathbf{R}, \quad \text{where} \quad u(s,j) := u_j(s_j) \quad \text{for} \quad j \in A. \tag{12}$$

The reward function generally depends on states and actions. In our particular migration framework we suppose that the migrant's reward, given state s and action j, is the utility the migrant can extract from living one period in country j.

The objective of the migrant is to find a migration strategy, that is, loosely speaking, a sequence of actions $a(t)$ $(a(t) \in A)$ such that the expected, discounted total reward

$$\sum_{t=0}^{T} \beta^t u\left(s(t), a(t)\right) \tag{13}$$

is maximized, where we suppose $\beta \in (0,1)$ for the discount factor throughout this monograph. In (13) the states $s(t)$ evolve according to the stochastic transition law $P\left(\cdot | s(t-1), a(t-1)\right)$ in time.

Before proceeding any further with the discussion of particular migration decision models it remains to specify the concept of **migration strategy**. As already mentioned before, we restrict ourselves to strategies that do not depend on the whole history of the decision process. We utilize so–called **Markov strategies** that depend only on the previous state $s \in S$. Mathematically a migration strategy σ is a sequence of (measurable) mappings

$$\sigma = (\sigma_0, \ldots, \sigma_T), \tag{14}$$

where

$$\sigma_t : S \to A$$

prescribes into which country to move for period $[t, t+1)$, depending on state $s(t)$. In some models below the same σ_t will be used for all periods. In this case we have a **stationary migration strategy**, that will be denoted simply by σ.

Now let there be given a general migration strategy $\sigma = (\sigma_0, \ldots, \sigma_T)$. This strategy induces a family of transition laws $\{P_t(\cdot|\cdot)\}_{t=0}^{T}$ that is given by $P_t(\cdot|s, \sigma_t(s))$ for all $t = 0, 1, \ldots, T$. It is well known from the theory of Markov processes (e. g. Loeve (1963)) that the family of transition laws generates a probability measure on $B(\bigotimes_{t=0}^{T} S)$, that is denoted by $P\sigma$ to emphasize its dependence on the underlying migration strategy σ. The Markov process on $\bigotimes_{t=0}^{T} S$ is completely determined if there is given an initial state $s_0 = \bar{s} \in S$. Now we can formulate the migrant's problem mathematically as follows.

Given an initial state $\bar{s}$ the migrant wants to choose the migration strategy σ^* that maximizes the expression

$$E_{P_\sigma}\left[\sum_{t=0}^{T} \beta^t u\left(\cdot, \sigma_t(\cdot)\right) | s_0 = s\right]. \tag{15}$$

If we consider stationary strategies σ then we obtain homogeneous Markov processes on the space $\left(\bigotimes_{t=0}^{T} S, B(\bigotimes_{t=0}^{T} S)\right)$. And the migrant has to choose a stationary strategy that maximizes (15).

I.3 Specializations of the General Model

I.3.1 The (General) Multi–Armed–Bandit ($\equiv$ MAB–) Model of International Migration and the 'Gittins–Index' Method

During the past 20 years considerable effort has been put into the application of sequential decision models to economic problems. Starting from the application of the elementary theory of Optimal Stopping to problems of job search and price search under incomplete information (e. g. McCall (1970), Gastwirth (1976), Rothschild (1973)), more refined decision models have been applied in recent years. In this context one has to mention first of all the "Gittins–index" method which can be regarded as a fruitful generalization of Optimal Stopping (see Gittins (1979), Whittle (1980), Berninghaus (1984)). Gittins–index theory can roughly be characterized as a solution method for determining the optimal strategy in a Markovian decision process with a very special structure, known in the literature under the name of **Multi–Armed–Bandit** processes.

Generally a MAB problem can be characterized as follows: a decision maker has, in each period, to pursue one of N independent projects or activities. These projects, on the other hand, are characterized by state spaces S_j ($j = 1, \ldots, N$) and transition probabilities $\Pi_j(B_j|s_j)$ ($B_j \in B(S_j)$) which control the state transitions from one period to another. If the state of a project at decision time point t is given by $s_j(t)$ and the individual decision maker decides to work on the j–th project in period $[t, t+1)$, the decision maker receives reward $u_j(s_j(t))$. It is crucial for the MAB problem that the states of the remaining projects are kept frozen during period $[t, t+1)$. Only the state of the project the decision maker is just working on changes from one period to the next.

Then it is the aim of the decision maker in a MAB problem to choose the sequencing of projects such that the expected total discounted reward is maximized. It is easy to see that a MAB process can be regarded as a specialized Markovian decision process.[8]

Now we will specify a model of a migration decision process which, as we claim, is highly relevant for capturing essential parts of the incomplete information aspects and can most appropriately be modelled by a MAB process. This model will be called the **MAB model of international migration**:

The potential migrant supposes that there are "true" but unknown characteristics C_j of each country remaining constant during the planning horizon of infinitely many periods $t = 1, 2, \dots, \infty$.

E. g. C_j could be – as in example 2 in I.2 – the "wage–quality of life" pair $C_j = (w_j, x_j)$. In the following let $s_j(t)$ denote the migrant's state of information about C_j at the beginning of period t.[9]

Obviously we have here the "state of information" interpretation of the state space in mind. Concerning the evolution of $s_j(t)$ in time the following important assumption has now to be made:

Only by living in country j in a period, his state of information about C_j may change. (16)

Assumption (16) is a specialized version of the crucial property of MAB processes that has been introduced above. The migrant who moved to country j in period t is supposed to expect a stochastic change of his states of information about country j according to the transition probability

$$\Pi_j : (B(S_j) \times S_j) \to [0, 1], \tag{17}$$

where we give the detailed interpretation of this concept immediately as follows

$\Pi_j(B_j|s_j) \equiv$ the migrant's subjective probability that his state of information about C_j will change to $s'_j \in B_j$ during period t, where at the beginning of that period his state of information was s_j **and** where he will live in j during that period. (18)

Finally, let the per period utility functions $u_j(\cdot) : S_j \to \mathbf{R}$ be given as in I.2 (for the "state of information"–interpretation). Then it remains to specify the global state transition law $P(\cdot|\cdot)$ for the induced Markovian decision process that has to be composed

[8] The construction of the state space S and the reward function $u(\cdot)$ is straightforward. The precise definition of the state transition law of the induced Markovian decision process will be given below.

[9] For ease of notation we identify from here on each period $[t, t+1)$ with its starting point t.

of the transition probabilities $\Pi_j(\cdot|\cdot)$ as follows.

$$P(B_1 \times \ldots \times B_N|s,j) := \left[\begin{array}{lll} \Pi_j(B_j|s_j) & \text{if} & s_{-j} \in B_{-j}, \\ 0 & \text{if} & s_{-j} \in B_{-j}, \end{array} \right. \tag{19}$$

for any $(B_1 \times \ldots \times B_N) \in B(S_1 \times \ldots \times S_N)$, $s = (s_1, \ldots, s_N) \in S$, where we use the notation

$$s_{-j} := (s1, \ldots, s_{j-1}, s_{j+1}, \ldots, s_N), \tag{20a}$$

$$B_{-j} := (B_1 \times \ldots \times B_{j-1} \times B_{j+1} \times \ldots \times B_N). \tag{20b}$$

This specification of the law of motion implies that for discrete state sets S_j only states $s' = (s'_1, \ldots, s'_N) \in S$ can be reached with positive probabilities from s, for which $s_{-j} = s'_{-j}$ holds. This corresponds to the assumption that in each period only one country can be visited by migration and that only the state of this country may change its characteristics in that period (compare (16)). Definition (19) now completes our description of the migration process (= MAB process) as a special Markovian decision process.

In chapt. I.3.2 we will analyse some special version of this scenario from an economic point of view. In the remaining part of this subsection we will briefly develop the Gittins–index method as a useful tool for characterising an optimal migration strategy in the general framework of a MAB migration model, as specified above.

The basic idea of the so–called Gittins–index policy is to reduce the solution of the MAB–migration problem to the solution of simpler (artificial) stopping problems. For this sake one has to consider, for each country j separately, the following stopping problem:

> $SP(s_j, Z_j)$: Suppose there is given a state of information $s_j \in S_j$ about country j and the migrant has the options to live in j for a further period and then proceeding optimally or to retire from this decision problem with a terminal payment $Z_j \in \mathbf{R}$. Then he has to decide whether to stop the decision process or to continue for at least a further period.

If we denote by $V_j(Z_j, s_j)$ the maximal expected discounted return of the problem $SP(s_j, Z_j)$ then we have the following functional equation[10]

$$V_j(Z_j, s_j) := \max\{Z_j; u_j(s_j) + \beta \int V_j(Z_j; \cdot) d\Pi_j(\cdot|s_j)\} \tag{21}$$

from wich we can in principle derive the optimal stopping strategy for the problems $SP(s_j, Z_j)$ for different $s_j \in S_j, Z_j \in \mathbf{R}$. We have only to compare the value of stopping immediately with the value of continuing at least one further period. That is, comparing the two terms in brackets on the right–hand side of equation (21). Obviously we will proceed optimally by pursuing the activity giving the larger value. We are not interested in determining this strategy here but we want to perform the following procedure: determine

[10] Again we assume the integral, which is taken over S_j, to exist.

the value of Z_j such that the migrant is **indifferent** between staying for a further period and retiring from the decision problem. Let us denote this value by $Z_j(s_j)$ to emphasize its state dependence. Formally we therefore get a mapping $Z_j : S_j \to \mathbf{R}$ where $Z_j(s_j)$ is given by the following equation:

$$Z_j(s_j) = u_j(s_j) + \beta \int V_j(Z_j(s_j), \cdot) d\Pi_j(\cdot | s_j). \tag{22}$$

The real numbers $Z_j(s_j)$ are called **"Gittins-indices"**. It can be demonstrated that in a MAB model as specified above, there always exists a unique solution of (22) (e. g. Berninghaus (1984)); therefore $Z_j(\cdot)$ is well-defined: given s_j, the Gittins-index $Z_j(s_j)$ can be calculated in principle from the functional equation (22) above.

Surprisingly the Gittins-indices turn out to be the central concepts in determining an optimal migration strategy. The following proposition is an application of corresponding theorems by Gittins (1979), and Whittle (1980):

Proposition I.3.1 *Let there be given the MAB migration problem as it has been described above. Furthermore let there be given a state of information $s = (s_1, \ldots, s_N)$ at the beginning of period t. Then the optimal migration strategy σ^* can be described as follows*

$$\sigma^*(s) := j^*, \quad \textit{where} \quad Z_{j^*}(s_{j^*}) = \max_{j \in \{1,\ldots,N\}} \{Z_j(s_j)\}.$$

In other words, the migrant moves in each period into the country that is characterized by the largest Gittins-index. If at any decision time point at least two countries have the same largest Gittins-index, some arbitrary tie-breaking rule may be applied. For example, in this case the migrant should move into the country which has a larger (or smaller) index.

Remarks:

a) As is well known from the theory of stochastic dynamic programming, without loss of generality the optimal strategy can be assumed to be a stationary one, since the Markovian decision process corresponding to the MAB-migration problem is stationary.

b) Although the Gittins-index policy considerably simplifies the calculation of the optimal policy, it may still be a difficult task to calculate $Z_j(s_j)$ explicitly in a given model.

c) It follows immediately from the above proposition that only the Gittins-index of the region where the migrant is living may change while the Gittins-indices of the other regions remain constant.

The proof of Proposition I.3.1. is not trivial (see e. g. Ross (1983), pp. 131-141). An illustrative proof of the validity of the Gittins-index rule has been given in a special framework by Berninghaus/Seifert-Vogt (1987). It is not the purpose of this chapter to analyse the proof of this important theorem. But nevertheless it might be useful to illustrate the intuitive plausibility of the Gittins–index rule by a simple example below before we apply the proposition to a more special MAB migration model in the following section.

Example

Let us consider a decision maker in a MAB framework who can choose pulling one of two arms at each decision time point. The first arm is deterministic in the sense that the decision maker obtains 5 monetary units per period if he pulls this arm. But he is incompletely informed about the return of the second arm. For the sake of simplicity we assume that the decision maker knows that the return of the second arm is equal to 0 with a priori probability 1/4 and equal to 10 with probability 3/4. But he has to pay $-c$ (with $0 < c < 7.5(\beta/(1-\beta))$) monetary units if he pulls the second arm for the first time. Furthermore after pulling this arm for the first time, the decision maker is supposed to know the return (either 10 or 0) with certainty.

Now we are ready to calculate the optimal policy according to the theorem by looking at equation (21) and (22) above. To determine the Gittins–index for the first arm we have to calculate $V_1(Z_1(\cdot), \cdot)$ which is obviously given by

$$V_1(Z_1(\cdot), \cdot) \equiv \max\left\{Z_1(\cdot), \frac{5}{1-\beta}\right\}$$

consequently we have

$$Z_1(\cdot) \equiv \frac{5}{1-\beta}.$$

It is a little bit more difficult to calculate the Gittins–index for the second arm as there is a state transition after the first pull of this arm. For ease of notation let us denote by

$$V_2(Z_2, s_0), \qquad V_2(Z_2, 0), \qquad V_2(Z_2, 10)$$

the value functions of pulling the second arm if arm 2 has not been pulled yet, if information on arm 2 has come in and implies that return on arm 2 is 0 or 10 respectively. According to (21) we have to solve the functional equation

$$V_2(Z_2, s_0) = \max\{Z_2(s_0), -c + \beta[\tfrac{1}{4}V_2(Z_2, 0) + \tfrac{3}{4}V_2(Z_2, 10)]\}. \tag{21'}$$

By the same reasoning as above we obtain

$$\begin{aligned} V_2(Z_2, 0) &= \max\{Z_2, 0\} \\ V_2(Z_2, 10) &= \max\left\{Z_2, \frac{10}{1-\beta}\right\} \end{aligned}$$

as the second arm gives a deterministic return from the second pull on. Consequently we determine $Z_2(s_0)$ from

$$Z_2(s_0) = -c + \beta\left[\tfrac{1}{4}\max\{Z_2(s_0), 0\} + \tfrac{3}{4}\max\left\{Z_2(s_0), \tfrac{10}{1-\beta}\right\}\right] \tag{22'}$$

which results in[11]

$$Z_2(s_0) = \frac{-c}{(1-\beta/4)} + 7,5\frac{\beta}{(1-\beta)(1-\beta/4)}.$$

Therefore it follows from the proposition that the decision maker will pull the unknown arm if $Z_2(s_0) > Z_1(s_0)$, that is, after some manipulations if the inequality

$$c < 7.5\frac{\beta}{1-\beta} - 5\frac{(1-\beta/4)}{1-\beta} \tag{23}$$

is valid. Inequality (23) can be interpreted such that the decision maker obviously tries out the uncertain arm if the "experimenting costs" (here equal to c) are "sufficiently" low. This seems to be a plausible procedure if we furthermore take account of the fact that $Z_2(0) = 0$, $Z_2(10) = 10/1-\beta$, implying that the decision maker will change the arm if it turns out to be inferior after pulling it once.

For sake of completeness let us compare this optimal procedure with the traditional Human Capital rule which requires arm 1 to be pulled at the beginning if

$$\frac{7,5\beta}{1-\beta} - \frac{5}{1-\beta} < c. \tag{24}$$

Combining inequality (24) with (23) we can see that there always exists a whole interval of c such that (23) and (24) are fulfilled simultaneously, or in other words, that the H. C. rule proposes a suboptimal procedure. Intuitively this result drastically illustrates the weakness of the H. C. rule (even in its modified version with expected values) which excludes rational learning.

I.3.2 Some Economic Implications of the Gittins–Index Policy

In this section we will specify the MAB migration model of the previous section by utilizing some special assumptions concerning the per period utility functions and the sequence of state transitions as it has already been given in section I.2. By this specification we obtain a migration model which is sophisticated enough to draw interesting conclusions concerning individual migration behaviour. On the other hand it is simple enough to be analytically tractable.

Again we consider a potential migrant who can choose to move into one of N countries. The true characteristic of a country j is supposed to consist of four components:

i) the wage w_j that can be earned in j,

ii) the moving costs k_j for moving into country j. They have to be interpreted here first of all as opportunity costs of search when moving to an unknown place (generated by gathering information about shopping facilities, schooling, housing etc.)

[11]The result is derived by setting primarily $Z_2(s_0) > \frac{10}{1-\beta}$ which implies $Z_2(s_0) = \frac{-c}{1-\beta}$, a contradiction. Consequently we have to assume $Z_2(s_0) \leq \frac{10}{1-\beta}$. From our restrictions concerning c we can furthermore exclude the case $Z_2(s_0) < 0$ which finally gives us the unique solution of equation (22').

iii) the search costs c_j that are generated by job search activities in country j and

iv) the quality of life in country j that is — to simplify considerations — supposed here to be representable by a real number x_j.[12]

Thus the characteristics C_j may be represented here by the quadruple $C_j = (w_j, x_j, c_j, k_j)$. For the sake of simplicity we assume that the migrant is completely informed about c_j and k_j ($j = 1, \ldots, N$) but is supposed to be incompletely informed about w_j and x_j. To be more precise, the migrant is supposed to have a subjective probability distribution over w_j and x_j with cumulative distribution functions denoted by $F_j(\cdot)$ and $G_j(\cdot)$. To improve his state of information a migrant is allowed to search actively for a job in the first period of his stay in j. Then he incurs search costs c_j and at the end of the period he knows w_j.

From a formal point of view the decision maker is allowed to draw in each country a random sample which is not costless, from the population of jobs distributed according to $F_j(\cdot)$. Naturally this is a rather crude picture of a job search process. One could incorporate more sophisticated job search models but this would make it only more difficult to get insight into the structure of the optimal migration policy. To connect our assumption here with the standard models of job search one could imagine for example that the distribution $F_j(\cdot)$ already results from performing some sophisticated job search strategy in country j.

Concerning the quality of life we suppose that the migrant knows his realized x_j at the end of the second period of his stay in country j. This seems to be a realistic assumption as we interprete x_j as comprising all the experience that a migrant makes after living for some time in j (making friends, discovering the "cultural environment" etc.). That is, we assume that x_j is essentially **belated information**. For the sake of simplicity we suppose furthermore that x_j can be measured in monetary units such that the total return on migration into country j after two periods of living there is completely known and given by $(w_j + x_j)$. Concentrating on a particular country j we can illustrate the return and information process by the following drawing.

[12]Compare I.2 for a more detailed discussion of this concept.

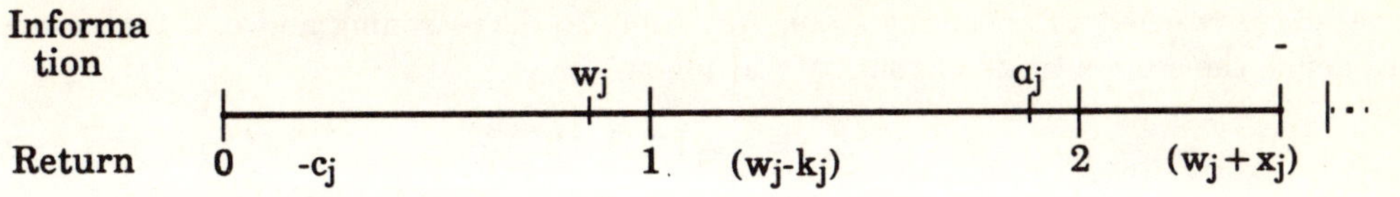

Figure 1: Information and return structure of the migration process

Obviously one could summarize the above procedure simply as follows. Before a potential migrant settles forever in an unknown country he spends the first period searching for a job. After having found a job the migrant can decide to move into the country for at least one period incurring moving costs k_j. At the end of the second period he is completely informed about all relevant aspects of the return in j and he will earn (w_j+x_j) in each future period. It should be emphasized here that the migrant has the opportunity to leave country j after each period to "try out" another country. Naturally this would make sense only at the beginning of the information gathering process in each country. Concerning the distributions $F_j(\cdot)$ and $G_j(\cdot)$ we could assume either that job search and experience of quality of life constitute random experiments whose results are governed by $F_j(\cdot)$ and $G_j(\cdot)$ or that these distributions only display the heterogenity between the migrants with respect to w_j and x_j. And the migrants do not exactly know to which w_j– and x_j-class they belong. Anyhow, the following derivations do not depend on the interpretations of $F_j(\cdot)$ and $G_j(\cdot)$. One only has to assume that from a formal point of view some steps in the migration history of a migrant are connected with the realization of random variables W_j and X_j whose distributions the migrants suppose to know. Furthermore these distributions also might differ from the **true** distributions denoted by $\bar{F}_j(\cdot)$ and $\bar{G}_j(\cdot)$ which will only play a role in later chapters of our book.

Next we will have to specify the state space. Here we can refer to our explanations already given in section I.2. Thus taking account of the fact that "no information" has also to be regarded as a state of information, we define, for each country, an artificial information state s_{0j} by

$$s_{0j} \quad \ldots \quad \text{"country } j \text{ has not been visited before".}$$

To motivate our particular definition of s_j we remind here of the information process caused by migration into country j, now supplemented by the information state s_{0j}, which can be illustrated by the following sketch.

$$s_{0j} \longrightarrow w_j \longrightarrow (w_j, x_j) \longrightarrow (w_j, x_j) \longrightarrow \ldots$$

If the decision maker decides to search for a job in country j his state of information changes from s_{0j} to $w_j (\in \mathbf{R})$ which induces a change from w_j to $(w_j, x_j) \in \mathbf{R}^2$ provided the decision maker decides to stay for a second period in country j. After this state of information has been reached it does not change anymore. Technically spoken the decision maker has reached an absorbing state. According to the reasoning above, it makes sense to define the state space[13] of country j as follows

$$S_j := \{s_{0j}\} \cup \mathbf{R} \cup \mathbf{R}^2. \tag{25}$$

Now we can describe state transitions more precisely by a stochastic transition law, that is, a transition probability on S_j, denoted by $\Pi_j(\cdot|\cdot)$ and represented by its cumulative distribution functions as follows

$$\begin{aligned} \Pi_j(w_j|s_{0j}) &:= F_j(w_j) \\ \Pi_j((w_j, x_j)|w_j) &:= G_j(x_j) \\ \Pi_j((w_j, x_j)|(w_j, x_j)) &:= 1. \end{aligned} \tag{26}$$

Obviously we need not consider other state transitions.

Up to now we have almost all ingredients to interprete the migration problem as a specialized Multi–armed Bandit problem. It remains to define the per period utility functions $u_j : S_j \rightarrow \mathbf{R}$ for each country that associates to each state in S_j an (economic) reward. According to our model presented above we define

$$\begin{aligned} u_j(s_{0j}) &:= -c_j, \\ u_j(w_j) &:= (w_j - k_j) \\ u_j((w_j, x_j)) &:= (w_j + x_j). \end{aligned} \tag{27}$$

Now we are ready to interprete "migrating into country j" as "pursuing activity j", characterized by $S_j, \Pi_j(\cdot|\cdot)$ and x_j, in a Multi–armed Bandit problem.[14] In our special problem the decision maker is rather efficient in gathering information. After pulling an arm twice he is already supposed to be completely informed about the return of this arm.

More sophisticated methods of information–gathering are conceivable. For example, complete information could come in after some periods according to a given probability distribution. Or one could assume that complete information will only be obtained "in the limit" after infinitely many periods. But we do not believe that our economic implications, to be derived below, would be changed considerably.

Next we will characterize the optimal migration strategy in this special MAB model. Using its structure as described in Proposition I.3.1 it can be characterized completely by the Gittins–indices. Consequently, in analysing further properties of the optimal policy we only have to analyse the properties of the Gittins–indices.

Primarily we can conclude from the model that there are only **three** indices relevant for the decision maker. More precisely, we need to consider only $Z_j(s_j)$ where s_j can take 3 types of states:

$$s_{0j} \longrightarrow w_j \longrightarrow (w_j, x_j)$$

[13]Technical remark: S_j should be regarded as a finite union of disjoint sets provided with its "final topology".

[14]Because of the definition of the transition probabilities given above we have a Multi–armed Bandit problem with "independent arms". The state transitions of one "arm" do not depend on the states of other "arms".

The following Proposition gives useful information concerning the determination of the Gittins–indices for our special MAB model.

Proposition I.3.2

a) Let there be given the state of information (w_j, x_j), then

$$Z_j(w_j, x_j) = \frac{w_j + x_j}{1-\beta} \tag{28}$$

b) let there be given the state of information (w_j), then $Z_j(w_j)$ is determined by

$$Z_j(w_j) = \frac{w_j - k_j}{1-\beta} + \frac{\beta}{1-\beta} \int \left(\frac{w_j + x_j}{1-\beta} - Z_j(w_j) \right)^+ dG_j(x_j) \tag{29}$$

c) let there be given no information about country j, then $Z_j(s_{0j})$ is determined by

$$\begin{aligned} Z_j(s_{0j}) \quad = \quad & \frac{-c_j}{(1-\beta)} + \beta \int \Big(w_j - k_j + \beta \int (\frac{w_j + x_j}{1-\beta} \\ & - Z_j(s_{0j}))^+ dG_j(x_j) - (1-\beta) Z_j(s_{0j}) \Big)^+ dF_j(w_j). \end{aligned} \tag{30}$$

Proof: See Appendix A.I.3.

To give a graphic illustration for determining Gittins indices let us denote the right–hand side[15] of equation (29) resp. (30) by $f_2(k, w, G(\cdot), Z)$ and $f_3(c, k, F(\cdot), G(\cdot), Z)$. Obviously $f_2(\cdot)$ and $f_3(\cdot)$ are non–increasing in Z. The Gittins–indices are determined from the intersection of the graphs of $f_2(\cdot)$ and $f_3(\cdot)$ with the 45°–line.

[15]For ease of notation we omit the index j whenever it is possible without confusion.

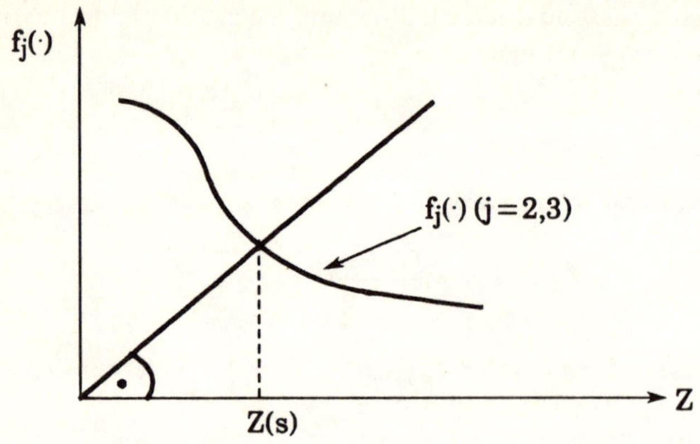

Figure 2: Determination of the Gittins–indices according to equation (29) and (30)

Here we exclude negative Gittins–indices from consideration by implicitly assuming that the support of $F_j(\cdot)$ and $G_j(\cdot)$ is "large enough".[16] [17] More precisely, we have to assume for each j

$$0 < w_j - kj + \beta \int \frac{(w_j + x_j)^+}{1-\beta} dG_j(x_j) \quad \forall \quad w_j \in \text{support } (F_j) \tag{31}$$

$$c_j < \beta \int \left[w_j - k_j + \beta \int \left(\frac{w_j + x_j}{1-\beta} \right)^+ dG_j(x_j) \right]^+ dF_j(w_j). \tag{32}$$

From the definition of $f_2(\cdot)$ and $f_3(\cdot)$ one can now derive the following conclusions (by shifting the graphs of these functions appropriately).

Proposition I.3.3

a) $Z_j(s_j)$ *is strictly decreasing in* c_j *and* k_j *resp., for* $s_j \neq (w_j, x_j)$,

b) $Z_j(w_j)$ *is strictly increasing in* w_j.

These conclusions can easily be seen to be correct by shifting the graph of $f_2(\cdot)$ and $f_3(\cdot)$ resp. to the left (for increasing k and c resp.) or shifting the graph of $f_2(\cdot)$ to the

[16]The "support" of $F_j(\cdot)$ is defined as the smallest closed set such that there is no probability mass on its complement.

[17]Negative Gittins-indices would arise if $f_j(\cdot, 0) < 0$, or in other words, if k_j resp. c_j are "large enough" compared with the support of $F_j(\cdot)$ resp. $G_j(\cdot)$.

right for increasing w). These results seem also to be intuitively plausible. For increasing moving costs and search costs the ranking of a country should not increase.

It is more important for the following development to analyse effects on the Gittins–indices that are induced by variations of $F_j(\cdot)$ resp. $G_j(\cdot)$. We are mainly interested in varying the distributions with respect to the "mean preserving spread". This is a well–known concept in the "Economics of uncertainty" (see for instance Rothschild/Stiglitz (1970)). Intuitively a probability distribution $F'(\cdot)$ has a larger m.p.s. than $F(\cdot)$ if it has the same expected value and $F'(\cdot)$ can be regarded as constructed from $F(\cdot)$ by shifting the mass of $F(\cdot)$ onto the tails. Consequently one can roughly say that $F'(\cdot)$ displays more variability than $F(\cdot)$.

Concerning m.p.s. one can now derive the following result

Proposition I.3.4 *Suppose $F_j'(\cdot)$ and/or $G_j'(\cdot)$ have a larger m.p.s. than $F_j(\cdot)$ and $G_j(\cdot)$ respectively, and let us denote the respective Gittins–indices by $Z_j'(s_{0j})$ and $Z_j(s_{0j})$ and $Z_j'(w)$ and $Z_j(w)$ respectively then we have*

$$Z_j'(s_{0j}) \geq Z_j(s_{0j})$$

$$Z_j'(w_j) \geq Z_j(w_j).$$

Proof :[18] See Appendix A.I.3.

Remark: It should be noticed here that this result utilizes **risk–neutrality** of the decision maker which has been assumed so far. In section I.4. we will show how the result of Proposition I.3.4. can be extended to particular classes of risk–averse decision makers.

The interpretation of the above result depends on the economic context which will be elaborated in more detail below. For the moment we should keep in mind the general interpretation that more variability in the wage and/or "quality of life" distribution increases the attractivity of a country. A plausible explanation for this result is due to the sequential character of the decision process. More variability in the relevant distributions implies more favourable results the decision maker can expect (and naturally more unfavourable results too). But as the decision maker can revise a decision after results turned out to be bad more variability may improve his expected pay–off.

Before we apply the results above to international migration we will derive a further property of the optimal migration policy in the following Proposition. This property connects our model with the well–known job search paradigm (e. g. Lippman/McCall (1976)) and furthermore simplifies the calculation of immigration and emigration rates as it will be clear at once.

Proposition I.3.5 *Suppose the migrant knows w_j after a job search process. Then he will stay in region j for at least one further period if $w_j \geq w_j^*$ where w_j^* is determined by*

[18]The proof is based on the fact that an integral $\int f(x)dF(x)$ increases for convex functions $f(\cdot)$ if $F(\cdot)$ has a larger m.p.s. (e. g. Lippman/McCall (1982)). As the integrands that appear in the integrals of $f_2(\cdot)$, $f_3(\cdot)$ obviously are convex functions (in w and x) the graphs of $f_2(\cdot)$ and $f_3(\cdot)$ are shifted to the right as a result of an increasing m.p.s.

the equation

$$k_j = w_j^* + \beta \int \left(\frac{w_j^* + \alpha_j}{1-\beta} - Z_j^* \right)^+ dG_j(\alpha_j) - (1-\beta) Z_j^*,$$

where $Z_j^* := \max_{i \neq j} Z_i(s_i)$, *and* $Z_i(s_i)$ *denotes the Gittins–index of country* i *depending on the state* s_i *that has been realized so far.*

Proof: See Appendix A.I.3.

Remark: Obviously w_j^* can be interpreted as reservation wage (in the sense of the traditional job search literature) for country j. In contrast to traditional job search models w_j^* depends on many parameters. It also depends on the Gittins–indices for the other countries. In other words, it depends on the state of information available about the remaining countries.

To summarize our results we can characterize the structure of the optimal migration policy in our model as follows. Suppose a potential migrant is at the beginning of the decision process: then he should

a) calculate the Gittins–index for each region, and go into the country with the largest index,

b) pay c_j and start a job search process; if $w_j < w_j^*$ search the country with the next highest index, if $w_j \geq w_j^*$ pay k_j and stay at least for another period in this country,

c) after realization of x_j calculate the Gittins–index for country j again; if it has become smaller than at least one of the other indices go into the country with the largest index, otherwise stay in country j.

This is the main result of chapter I. The optimal migration policy is derived directly from the Gittins–index policy for the MAB migration problem that has been given in detail in the previous propositions.

We will terminate section I.3.2. by drawing some implications from our previous results that seem to be most relevant for the theory of migration and its applications. By modelling the migration problem within a sequential decision framework we are able to give more satisfying explanations for some empirically relevant observations as it can be shown below.

1ST IMPLICATION:

> *A country becomes more attractive for migration if the information about the non–pecuniary return*[19] x_j *decreases.*

This is at first glance a paradoxical result that is based on Proposition I.3.4 and an appropriate definition of the concept "less informed" that will be given immediately. Let

[19]It is easy to see that a similar conclusion is valid for monetary returns provided we assume incomplete information about the monetary returns.

us consider a potential migrant who is incompletely informed about x_j. We can formalize this by the assumption that the migrant regards non–pecuniary returns as a random variable x_j. Then it is natural to say that the migrant is less informed about the non-pecuniary returns if there is more "noise" in X_j. To formalize this idea we would say that a migrant is less informed if he regards non–pecuniary returns as another random variable X_j', where[20]

$$X_j' \stackrel{d}{=} X_j + \epsilon \tag{33}$$

with $E(\epsilon|X_j) = 0$. Here ϵ can be interpreted as "noise" added to X_j.

Now we will connect this concept of information with the mean preserving spread. It follows from a well-known result (e. g. Rothschild/Stiglitz (1970), Theorem 2) that the distribution of a random variable X_j' has a larger "mean preserving spread" than X_j iff there is a "noise" variable ϵ with the properties noted in (33). That is, we can interprete the mean preserving spread of a distribution also as a measure of information contained in a distribution. Consequently we can conclude from Prop. I.3.4 that less information about X_j or equivalently a larger mean preserving spread increases the Gittins–index of a country and therefore the attractivity of a country, what is essentially the content of the first implication above.

The economic motivation behind this result rests on risk–neutrality together with the sequential strategy concept. For a distribution with a large mean preserving spread roughly promises large gains and losses simultaneously. Consequently a potential migrant may act optimally if he enters the countries with large mean preserving spreads at first. If he realizes a loss the migrant has the opportunity to remigrate as he is allowed to revise his decision later on. And, as he is supposed not to be risk–averse, the migrant decides to take these risks. This seems to be a stylized migration process which fits very well into the picture of immigration from Europe to the U. S. during the past centuries. In the following section we will show that implication 1 is valid even for risk-averse migrants who are "almost risk neutral" in a well defined sense.

2ND IMPLICATION:

Countries with high immigration have high emigration.

This is a well–known result that can be found in many empirical studies on internal migration (see e. g. Greenwood (1975), Pessino (1988)). As there are many institutional restrictions for international migration one need not expect this finding in international migration as well. Unfortunately we did not find empirical studies in international migration supporting this implication. But nevertheless let us explain the mechanism producing this implication within the framework of our model:[21] According to Prop. I.3.4 high immigration into a country may be generated by a distribution of X_j with a large "mean

[20] $X \stackrel{d}{=} Y$ iff the random variables X and Y have the same distribution.

[21] For this explanation to make sense we have to suppose additionally that the quality of life is a random variable X_j whose objective probability distribution is anticipated approximately by the potential migrant.

preserving spread". On the other hand such a distribution also induces higher realization probability of "low values" for x_j what may induce remigration. To be more precise we have

$$Z_j(w_j, x_j) = \frac{w_j + x_j}{1 - \beta}$$

for the Gittins–index with complete information about country j. Therefore we can see that the migrant will leave this country if x_j is low enough. This will happen more often if the distribution of X_j has a larger mean preserving spread. To summarize, we can roughly say that large immigration rates will be correlated with large emigration rates if the attractivity of a country is based on a large "mean preserving spread".

3RD IMPLICATION:

Remigration may be part of the optimal migration policy.

This is in contrast to almost all traditional microeconomic migration models which do not take account of incomplete information. According to these models remigration takes place if the decision maker made an error in his calculations. Then the migrant has to start his calculations anew. Whereas in our framework remigration will always be optimal if the Gittins–index of a country drops below the Gittins–index of the home country after living one period in this country.

Concerning the statements in the 2nd and 3rd implication we see that the empirical relevant phenomena expressed there can be explained satisfactorily within the context of our dynamic stochastic decision model. This supports our view that an essentially dynamic phenomenon as migration has to be captured by a stochastic dynamic decision model.

Prop. I.3.3, I.3.4 and the 1st implication describe essentially **comparative static properties** of the optimal migration policy. To summarize, we can briefly say that a country becomes more attractive for immigration if the wage rate increases resp. if the migration costs decrease (Proposition I.3.3). This result could be obtained also in the traditional Human Capital model for migration. Furthermore the attractivity of a country increases if information (in the sense defined above) about the country decreases (Prop. I.3.4). This interesting result is derivable only in a framework in which incomplete information can be described adequately.

I.4 Risk–Averse Migrants in the Special MAB Migration Model

In this section we consider once more the special MAB migration model specified in I.3.2. Our main concern will be to analyse the robustness of Proposition I.3.4 and its implications 1 and 2 in the last section, if the assumption of a risk neutral migrant is relaxed.

We are especially interested here in elaborating conditions under which our (at a first glance) "paradoxical result" can be extended to risk–averse migrants. This analysis is not a merely technical extension, but it is highly relevant for explaining migration phenomena, as many potential migrants are expected to be risk–averse decision makers.

We restrict our analysis to uncertainty about the quality of life index x[22], i.e. we consider a situation where the migrant's state of information about the country in question is given by the wage rate $s = w$. Without loss of generality we may then assume the search costs c to be $= 0$. The relevant dates about the country are

- the wage rate w
- the migration costs k
- the migrants p.d.f. $G(\cdot)$ concerning x.

The migrant's per period utility function u is now given by

$$u(s) = \left[\begin{array}{ll} w - k, & \text{if} \quad s = w \\ w + v(x), & \text{if} \quad s = (w, x) \end{array} \right. \tag{34}$$

where $v : X \to \mathbf{R}$, $X \subset \mathbf{R}$, is an increasing concave (and – for technical reasons – twice differentiable) von–Neumann–Morgenstern utility function such that the migrant's preferences on the set of probability distributions $G(\cdot)$ on the set X of possible values of the quality of life index x can be represented by the expected utility function $\tilde{v}(\cdot)$ with

$$\tilde{v}(G) = \int_X v(x) dG(x) \tag{35}$$

As it can be easily seen from the proof of Prop. I.3.2 the relevant Gittins–index $Z(w)$ for the state of information $s = w$ is now determined by the functional equation

$$Z(w) = \frac{w - k}{1 - \beta} + \frac{\beta}{1 - \beta} \int_X \left[\frac{w + v(x)}{1 - \beta} - Z(w) \right]^+ dG(x) \tag{36}$$

i.e. the determination of the Gittins–index remains the same for the more general type of utility function, but its value depends on the specification of $v(\cdot)$. Since we deal in the present section with a comparative static analysis of the Gittins–index $Z(w)$ for different $v(\cdot)$, k and $G(\cdot)$, whereas w will be held fixed, we will write here

$$Z(w) = Z(v, k, G), \tag{37}$$

to emphasize the interesting dependencies.

The proof of Prop. I.3.4 is based on the argument that for linear utility functions $v(\cdot)$, i.e. for risk–neutral migrants, the integrand in (36) can be shown to be convex. Obviously for concave non–linear utility functions $v(\cdot)$ the convexity of the integrand will in general not be given any longer. And therefore we cannot be sure that for a mean preserving

[22] In the following we will omit the country index j since we will only consider one fixed country.

spread $G'(\cdot)$ of $G(\cdot)$ the right–hand side of (36) will shift upwards such that the relation $Z(v,k,G') \geq Z(v,k,G)$ would hold.

We will proceed now as follows

a) First we will try, by precise mathematical reasoning, to confirm the intuition that the conclusion of Prop. I.3.4 will remain valid if the degree of risk–aversion is "small" in a well defined sense that will be specified in the following proposition.

Proposition I.4.1 *Let $G(\cdot)$ and $k \geq 0$ be given, and let (v_n) be a sequence of $G(\cdot)$–integrable functions $v_n : X \to \mathbf{R}$, where we have for all n:*

$$v_n \quad \textit{is concave,} \tag{38}$$

$$v_{n+1}(x) \geq v_n(x) \quad \forall x \quad \textit{and} \tag{39}$$

$$\lim_{n\to\infty} v_n(x) = v^*(x) \quad \forall x, \quad \textit{with } v^* \textit{ linear} \tag{40}$$

Then for the sequence of Gittins–indices $\left[Z^{(n)}\right]_{n=1}^{\infty}$ with $Z^{(n)} := Z(v_n,k,G)$ the relation

$$\lim_{n\to\infty} Z^{(n)} = Z^* := Z(v^*,k,G) \tag{41}$$

holds.

Proof: Appendix A.I.4

As an example for a sequence (v_n) fulfilling the conditions (38), (39) and (40) consider the following sequence of utility functions

$$v_n(x) := -e^{-nx} + bx, \quad \text{where} \quad b > 0.$$

The economic implication of the proposition I.4.1 is the following. If a migrant has a risk–averse utility function $v_n(\cdot)$ which does not differ too much from the utility function $v^*(\cdot)$ of a risk–neutral migrant, and if a country becomes more attractive for the v^*–migrant because of a m.p.s. of $G(\cdot)$ then this higher attractivity will also result for the v_n–migrant in spite of his risk aversion, provided n is "large enough".

Proposition I.4.1 is a typical limit theorem whose result is rather crude. Especially if we consider a particular risk–averse potential migrant characterized by a given concave utility function $v(\cdot)$, we would be interested in his migration behaviour in face of an increasing "mean–preserving spread" in the distribution of x.

b) In the next step we will therefore analyse the decision problem of a particular risk–averse migrant in face of increasing uncertainty. More precisely, we will keep the utility function of the migrant fixed but we will vary his migration costs k to answer the question whether there exists a range of migration costs such that even the risk–averse migrant will prefer to go into a more risky country. We are able to derive an exact characterization of this critical set of migration costs depending on the "degree of uncertainty" in the distribution function $G(\cdot)$.

For this sake we will simplify our model a little bit. That is, to get a simpler measure for the degree of uncertainty we restrict our analysis here to the case where G belongs to the family of rectangular p.d.f. (G_ϵ) $\epsilon > 0$ of the form

$$G_\epsilon(x) := \begin{bmatrix} 0, & x < \bar{x} - \epsilon \\ \frac{x-\bar{x}+\epsilon}{2\epsilon}, & \bar{x} - \epsilon \leq \bar{x} < \bar{x} + \epsilon \\ 1, & \bar{x} + \epsilon \leq x \end{bmatrix} \quad (42)$$

with some fixed $\bar{x} \in X := \mathbf{R}$.[23] For $\epsilon = 0$ we set

$$G_0(x) := \begin{bmatrix} 1 & x \geq \bar{x} \\ 0 & x < \bar{x} \end{bmatrix} \quad (42')$$

that is, $G_0(\cdot)$ denotes the distribution function of the probability measure that is concentrated in x. Then it seems natural to use the number ϵ as a measure of the degree of uncertainty of the p.d.f. $G = G_\epsilon$ (it should be noticed that $\bar{x}$ will be held fixed in the following).

Since a von–Neumann–Morgenstern utility function is determined uniquely only up to positive affin–linear transformations, we may suppose without loss of generality that each utility function v we will consider satisfies the restriction

$$v(\bar{x}) = 0. \quad (43)$$

In this framework we will now try to characterize for fixed $v(\cdot)$ the set

$$C_v := \{(\epsilon, k) \in \mathbf{R}^2_{++} | Z_v(k, \epsilon) > Z_v(k, 0)\} \quad (44)$$

where we use the notation

$$Z_v(k, \epsilon) := Z(v, k, G_\epsilon). \quad (45)$$

I.e. for migration costs k and degrees of uncertainty ϵ such that $(\epsilon, k) \in C_v$ the attractivity of the country for immigration will increase, if the p.d.f. $G(\cdot)$ above x changes from $G = G_0$ to $G = G_\epsilon$, i.e. if there is uncertainty of degree ϵ instead of certainty about x. Next we will show that the set C_v can be represented by a connected subset of $\mathbf{R}^2_{++}$ whose upper boundary is given by the graph of an increasing function $K_v(\cdot)$.

Proposition I.4.2 *If $v(\cdot)$ is concave and non–linear, then there is a function $K_v : \mathbf{R}_{++} \rightarrow \mathbf{R}_+$ with*

$$K_v(\cdot) \quad \textit{increasing and} \quad (46)$$

$$\lim_{\epsilon \rightarrow 0} K_v(\epsilon) = 0 \quad (47)$$

such that C_v can be written as

$$C_v = \{(\epsilon, k) \in \mathbf{R}^2_{++} | k < K_v(\epsilon)\}. \quad (48)$$

---

[23]To avoid technical detail problems arising from the fact that the support of G_ϵ need not belong to X, if $X \subset \mathbf{R}$, we assume here $X = \mathbf{R}$.

The function $K_v(\cdot)$ determines the critical cost level of migration costs $K_v(\epsilon)$ for each degree of uncertainty ϵ, such that for migration costs $k < K_v(\epsilon)$ the country under uncertainty ϵ is more attractive for immigration than under certainty. For linear $v(\cdot)$ – the case considered in Prop. I.3.4 – the function $K_v(\cdot)$ exists too and is given by the limiting case $K_v(0) = 0$ and $K_v(\epsilon) = +\infty$ for $\epsilon > 0$.

A graphic illustration of the representation in the proposition is given below.

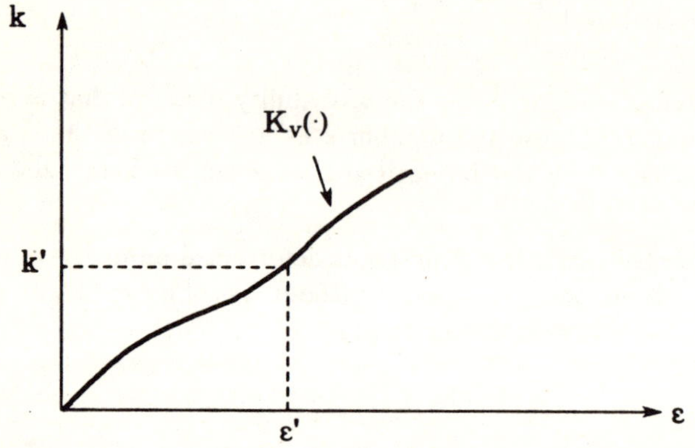

Figure 3: Illustration of the set C_v

Here C_v is given by the set strictly below the graph of $K_v(\cdot)$. We could interprete the situation also in the following sense. Suppose a risk–averse migrant is characterized by $v(\cdot)$ and migration costs k'; then the degree of uncertainty in the distribution $G(\cdot)$ has to be at least ϵ' such that the migrant will prefer uncertainty instead of certainty. In other words, the risk–averse migrant has to be compensated by the chance of a considerable improvement of his quality of life (which also implies a considerable possible detoriation of his present situation) to accept uncertainty. But one should be careful with this interpretation as $K_v(\cdot)$ might be bounded from above. In this case our interpretation would be valid only for sufficiently low k.

The proof of the proposition rests upon several lemmas whose proofs will be given in the appendix. As some of them are of independent interest for the illustration of the underlying economic problem we will cite them completely.

Lemma I.4.1 *Let for $\epsilon \geq 0$ $f_\epsilon : \mathbf{R} \to \mathbf{R}$ be the function describing the right–hand side of (36) for $G = G_\epsilon$, i.e. $f_\epsilon(\cdot)$ is given by*

$$f_\epsilon = \frac{w-k}{1-\beta} + \frac{\beta}{1-\beta} \int_{\bar{x}-\epsilon}^{\bar{x}+\epsilon} \left[\frac{w+v(x)}{1-\beta} - z \right]^+ dG_\epsilon(x) \qquad (49)$$

Then $f_\epsilon(\cdot)$ is continuous and decreasing for $z < z^+(\epsilon)$ and constant $= (w-k)/(1-\beta)$ for $z \geq z^+(\epsilon)$, where $z^+(\epsilon)$ is given by $v(x+\epsilon) = z^+(\epsilon)(1-\beta) - w$.

Proof: See Appendix A.I.4.

The shape of $f_\epsilon(\cdot)$ as described by this lemma may be graphically illustrated as follows.

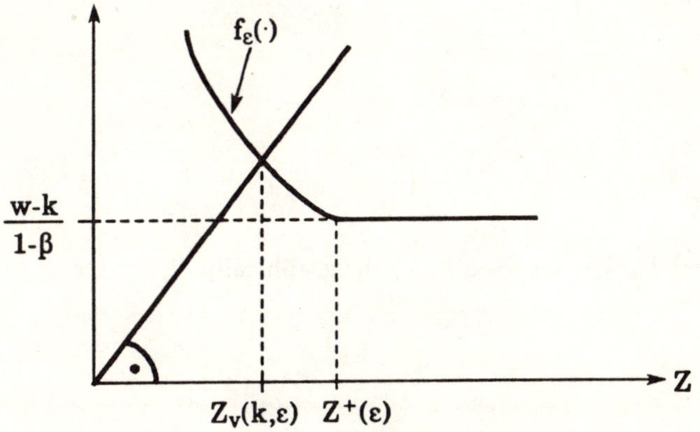

Figure 4: The graph of $f_\epsilon(\cdot)$

Then we can represent the Gittins–index, given (k,ϵ), as the projection of the intersection between the $f_\epsilon(\cdot)$–curve and the 45°–line onto the z–axis. That is, we obtain the following equation for the determination of the Gittins–index $Z_v(k,\epsilon)$

$$Z_v(k,\epsilon) = f_\epsilon(Z_v(k,\epsilon)). \tag{50}$$

Especially it follows from (49), (50), and our convention $v(\bar{x}) = 0$:

$$Z_v(k,0) = \frac{w}{1-\beta} - k. \tag{51}$$

In the next lemma there is given a powerful method for simplifying the comparison of Gittins–indices for arbitrary utility functions $v(\cdot)$ and different ϵ.

Lemma I.4.2 $\forall k > 0 : Z_v(k,\epsilon) \gtreqless Z_v(k,0) \Leftrightarrow f_\epsilon(Z_v(k,0)) \gtreqless Z_v(k,0)$

Proof: See Appendix A.I.4.

Thus we can obtain statements about the relation between $Z_v(k,\epsilon)$ and $Z_v(k,0)$ by analysing the relation of $f_\epsilon(Z_v(k,0)) = Z_v(k,0)$, i.e. without explicitly using the Gittins–index $Z_v(k,\epsilon)$, which to compute would not be an easy task for general v. Now it follows from (49) and (51)

Lemma I.4.3 *We can write:*

$$f_\epsilon(Z_v(k,0)) = Z_v(k,0) + \frac{\beta}{(1-\beta)^2} H_v(k,\epsilon) \tag{52}$$

with

$$H_v(k,\epsilon) := \int_{\bar{x}-\epsilon}^{\bar{x}+\epsilon} h_v(k,x)\,dG_\epsilon(x) \tag{53}$$

where h_v is defined by

$$h_v(k,x) := \left[\begin{array}{ll} -k(1-\beta), & x \leq x_k \\ v(x) & x > x_k \end{array} \right. \tag{54}$$

with x_k given by

$$v(x_k) = -k(1-\beta) \tag{55}$$

Proof: See Appendix A.I.4.

The functions $h_v(k,\cdot)$ and $H_v(k,\cdot)$ for fixed k may be graphically illustrated as follows

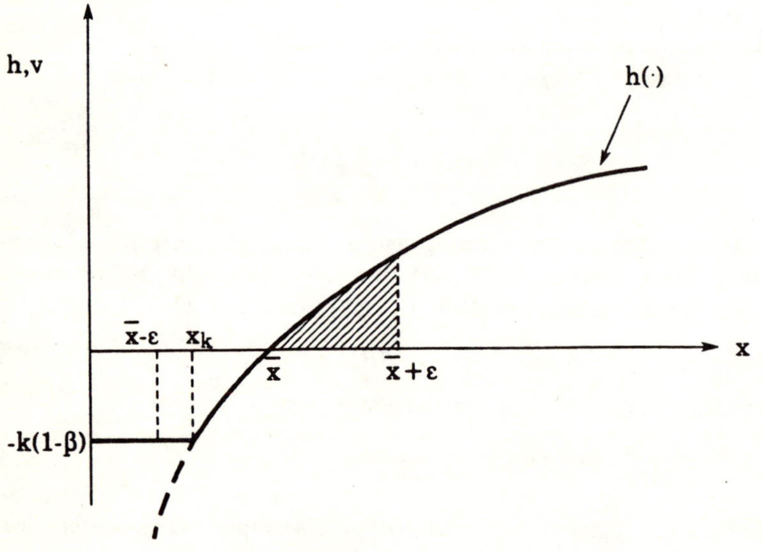

Figure 5: Graph of $h(\cdot)$

Therefore we get by combining (52), Lemma I.4.2., and (44)

$$C_v = \left\{ (\epsilon,k) \in \mathbf{R}_+^2 | H_v(k,\epsilon) > 0 \right\}. \tag{56}$$

Since $v(\bar{x}-\epsilon) \geq -k(1-\beta) = v(x_k)$ iff $\bar{x}-\epsilon \geq x_k$ it follows, because of the strict concavity of v (by Jensen's inequality), that for (ϵ,k) with $v(\bar{x}-\epsilon) \geq -k(1-\beta)$ we have

$H_v(k, \epsilon) < 0$. Thus the bordering line $\{(\epsilon, k) \in \mathbf{R}_+^2 | H_v(k, \epsilon) = 0\}$ is contained in the set $\{(\epsilon, k) \in \mathbf{R}_+^2 | v(\bar{x} - \epsilon) < -k(1 - \beta)\}$. Obviously we get for (ϵ, k) in the latter set:

$$H_v(\cdot, \epsilon) \quad \text{is decreasing in } k. \tag{57}$$

In order to derive the characterization of C_v in proposition I.4.2. it suffices to show

Lemma I.4.4 *There is a function $K_v : \mathbf{R}^+ \to \mathbf{R}^+$ such that*

$$H_v(K_v(\epsilon), \epsilon) = 0 \quad \forall \epsilon > 0 \tag{58}$$

that fulfills the requirements (46) and (47) of the Prop. I.4.2.

Proof: See Appendix A.I.4.

$k < K_v(\epsilon)$ is equivalent to $H_v(k, \epsilon) > 0$ (because of (57)), and thus by (56) it follows (48). As remarkable but simple consequences of the Lemmata I.4.2 and I.4.3 we obtain

Corollary I.4.1 *For $\epsilon > 0$ and migration costs $k \geq -v(\bar{x} - \epsilon)/(1 - \beta)$ the inequality $Z_v(k, 0) > Z_v(k, \epsilon)$ holds, i.e. the country is more attractive for immigration in the certainty case than in the case of an uncertainty of degree ϵ.*

Corollary I.4.2 *If the migration costs vanish, i.e. $k = 0$, then $Z_v(k, \epsilon) > Z_v(k, 0)$ $\forall \epsilon > 0$, i.e. uncertainty of degree ϵ about the country is more favourable for immigration than complete certainty about it.*

The result of the latter corollary emphasizes the importance of the sequential decision–framework: interpreting k as cost of information gathering it shows that a migrant will always be better off (ex–ante) by migration to the country in the uncertainty case than in the certainty case, because he can costlessly try out the quality of living there. If migration turns out to be successful, i.e. a value $x > 0$ has realized, he has gained ex–post, whereas if it turns out to be unsuccessful, i.e. if $x < 0$ has realized, he can remigrate such that in this unfavourable case he has nothing lost ex–post compared with the option of not migrating at all.

Let us terminate paragraph b) with a further result which can easily be derived along the lines of argument we used here:

Proposition I.4.3 *For migration costs k, and degrees of uncertainty $\epsilon_1 > \epsilon_2$, such that*

$$-v(\bar{x} - \epsilon_1)/(1 - \beta) \leq k$$

(i.e. a fortiori $-v(\bar{x} - \epsilon_2)/(1 - \beta) \leq k$) the inequality $Z_v(k, \epsilon_2) > Z_v(k, \epsilon_1)$ holds, i.e. the country is more attractive with uncertainty of degree ϵ_2 than with uncertainty of the greater degree ϵ_1.

The interpretation of the result is similar to corollary I.4.1. If migration costs are sufficiently large, what is made precise by the inequality in the corollary and proposition I.4.3, then a risk-averse potential migrant will be deterred from migration if uncertainty about the country increases sufficiently. One should keep in mind that all these considerations are valid for a given concave utility function.

c) In the present paragraph we will relax the assumption of a fixed utility function $v(\cdot)$. We are interested in the optimal migration behaviour of a potential migrant depending on his degree of risk-aversion. More specifically: using the framework outlined at the beginning of b), we fix ϵ, and are interested in the behaviour of the critical cost value $K_v(\epsilon)$ for utility functions $v(\cdot)$ with varying degrees of local absolute risk-aversion. For this sake we consider a family $\{v(\cdot;\alpha)\}\ \alpha \geq 0$ of (again increasing twice-differentiable) utility functions $v(\cdot,\alpha) : \mathbf{R} \to \mathbf{R}$, such that $v(x,\cdot)$ is partially differentiable with respect to α. Furthermore we assume (43) $v(\overline{x},\alpha) = 0$ to hold for all $\alpha \geq 0$ and furthermore:[24]

$$\frac{\partial\left(-\frac{v''(x,\alpha)}{v'(x,\alpha)}\right)}{\partial\alpha} > 0 \quad \forall x \tag{59}$$

and

$$\int_{x_{k,\alpha}}^{\overline{x}+\epsilon} \frac{\partial v(x,\alpha)}{\partial\alpha} dx < 0 \quad \forall k \geq 0, \tag{60}$$

where $x_{k,\alpha}$ is given by: $v(x_{k,\alpha},\alpha) = -k(1-\beta)$. Relation (59) says that the family $\{v(\cdot,\alpha)\}_{\alpha\geq 0}$ is parametrized in such a way that the Arrow–Pratt measure for local absolute risk-aversion of $v(\cdot,\alpha)$ is positively related to α. The meaning of (60) is illustrated graphically below.

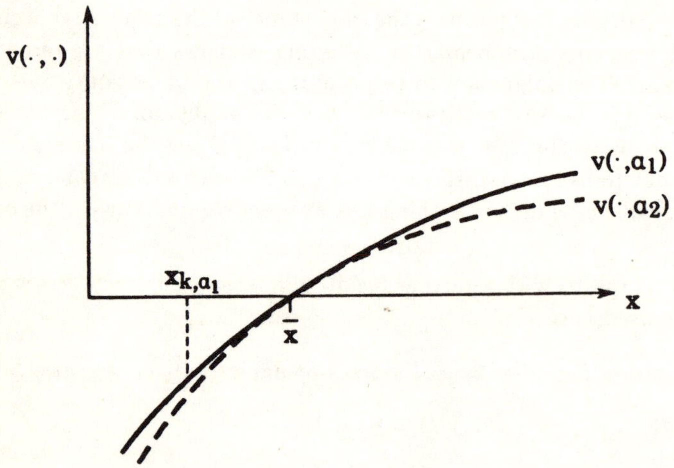

Figure 6: Different utility functions for $\alpha_1 < \alpha_2$.

Loosely speaking, $v(\cdot,\alpha_2)$ is more concave than $v(\cdot,\alpha_1)$ for $\alpha_2 > \alpha_1$. Therefore (60) implies that the "degree of concavity" (in this loose sense) is increasing in α.

[24]Here $v'(\cdot)$ and $v''(\cdot)$ denote the first and second derivative of v with respect to x.

Then it can be shown that the following result is true.

Proposition I.4.4 *Given a p.d.f.* $G(\cdot) = G_\epsilon(\cdot)$ *according to (42), with fixed* $\epsilon > 0$*, about the quality-of-life-index* x *in a country, and a family of utility functions* $\{v(\cdot, \alpha)\}_{\alpha \geq 0}$ *about* x *such that (43), (59) and (60) hold. Then the critical costs* $K(\epsilon, \alpha) := K_v(\cdot, \alpha)(\epsilon)$ *are decreasing in* α.

Proof: Appendix A.I.4.

The interpretation of Proposition I.4.4 is straightforward and the result is intuitively plausible. Roughly said, a more risk-averse migrant is not willing so much to move into a country with uncertain quality of life as a less risk-averse migrant. Technically speaking, the graph of the function of critical migration costs will be pulled down as it is shown in the drawing below.

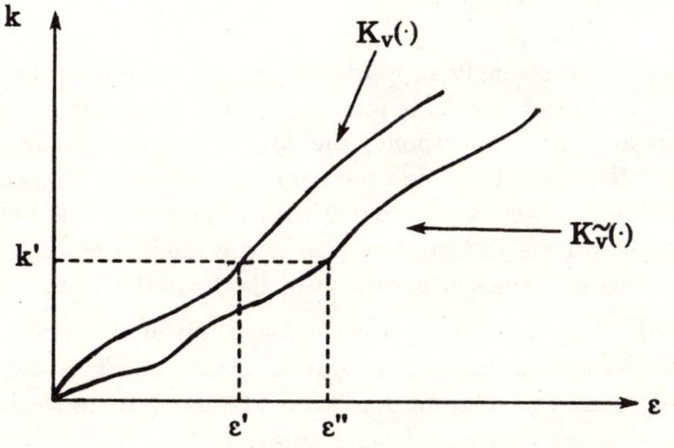

Figure 7: Graphs of $K_v(\cdot)$ for $v(\cdot)$ displaying differing degrees of risk-aversion

Let $\tilde{v}(\cdot)$ denote the utility function of an individual displaying more risk-aversion than $v(\cdot)$; then uncertainty for a migrant, characterized by migration costs k', has to be higher for a more risk-averse individual to induce immigration.

To summarize, we can support our statement that more uncertainty (and less information) about the relevant variables in a country increases its attractivity not only for risk-neutral but also (in a well defined sense) for risk-averse migrants. As this result is obviously not true for all risk-averse migrants its precise formulation needs some technical elaboration that has been done in the previous paragraphs a)–c).

Chapter II

Temporary vs. Permanent Migration

II.1 Introductory Remarks

The following phenomenon has been strongly supported by empirical observations (e.g. König (1986), Piore (1979)): a migrant typically is planning only a temporary stay in the host country (3-6 years). But actually he postpones the date of return such that remigration becomes less probable after some time. In other words, temporary migration has turned into permanent migration. As well-known empirical examples for this behaviour we can cite here guest-worker migration in Germany (see König (1986)) or immigration from Middle- and South-America into the southern part of the United States.

Without difficulties it would be possible to give an explanation of this phenomenon by using the special MAB model of international migration of chap. I.3: according to this model we could conclude that the migrant has been attracted to move into the host-country by high wage income expectations despite unfavourable expectations about the quality of life index. But whereas the wage expectation could be confirmed (by observation) the actual quality of life turned out to be significantly better such that 'staying in the host-country' would be the optimal choice.

Results from questionnaires show that this explanation is not very satisfactory for a great portion of guest-worker migration (see again König (1986)).

A different and in our opinion more satisfactory explanation has been given by Piore (1979) who concluded from empirical observations that most migrants are so-called target-savers. That means, they are planning to get into a host-country for the sake of saving money for investment in the home-country after remigration. According to these observations, a target-saver typically knows exactly how much capital he needs for opening a small grocery store, a café etc. before he migrates. And he expects to be able to accumulate the capital by migration. But as he is incompletely informed about the future economic development in the host-country and in the home-country as well it may turn out that he has to prolong the duration of his stay unexpectedly. For example, inflationary or deflationary tendencies in the host-country, unemployment and other unexpected economic events could prevent the target–saver from hitting his target within the planned period.

In this chapter we want to give a precise formalization of the target–saving argument within a microeconomic decision model. The framework of a sequential decision model of international migration as developed in chap. I.2 will turn out to be sufficient provided some appropriate modifications are made. First, in chap. II.2, we try to specify a general temporary– vs. permanent–migration model, and to characterize economic conditions in a two–country world which produce this phenomenon. Furthermore, in chap. II.3, we specialize the general model which enables us to obtain a formal derivation of the above–cited target–saver explanation for the temporary– vs. permanent -migration phenomenon.

II.2 A General Temporary– vs. Permanent–Migration Model with Target–Saving

In this section we will present a sequential decision process with a finite planning horizon $T > 1$, which is intended to capture the idea of target–saving as an explanation for the temporary– vs. permanent–migration phenomenon in rather general terms. Since we want to model a saving process, it seems to be urgent – in contrast to the models analyzed in chap. I – to specify consumption decisions explicitly, in addition to migration/remigration decisions.

We consider a two–country world, where the index 1 (rsp. 2) stands for the home (rsp. host) country. The first two periods $t = 0$ and $t = 1$ will be assumed to have very special features in our model which will be described below. In the remaining "typical" periods $t = 2, \ldots, T$ the possible choices for the decision maker consist of two components provided he is still in country 2 at the beginning of period t

- j : decision to live in country j ($\in \{1, 2\}$) during period t
- c : decision to consume c units of an aggregate consumption good during period t.

If the decision maker is living in country 1 at the beginning of t (≥ 2), then his choice possibilities will be restricted only to a consumption decision c in country 1 during period t; i. e. he will have no migration option in this case. This restriction is only relevant after remigration from the guest–country; thus we are concentrating on those cases where a guest–worker, in planning the duration of his stay abroad, considers the possibility of repeated (re)migration as irrelevant.

Now let us turn to the first two extraordinary periods. In period 0 only a migration decision is allowed, whereas in period 1 only a consumption decision in that country where the individual decided to migrate in period 0 is available. – The analytical reason for this separate treatment of periods 0 and 1 is that only by this an essential part of the incomplete information aspect can be captured. To facilitate intuition the reader should imagine period 0 as relatively short compared with the remaining periods. Furthermore the restriction in period 1 to a consumption decision is only relevant if the migrant has decided to migrate to country 2 in period 0. But in this case it does not seem to be too restrictive to exclude the possibility of immediate remigration. One could imagine for example that the guest–worker is bound by a labor contract to stay at least for one further period in the host–country.

Next let us denote by $x_j(t)$ the nominal money assets of the migrant in country j at the beginning of period t. To simplify the formal analytics we suppose that assets from country 2 to country 1 can only be transferred if the guest–worker remigrates; more precisely, if the individual is still living in country 2 at the beginning of period t, endowed with assets $x_2(t)$, and if he has no assets accumulated in country 1 before period t then his assets in country 1 at the beginning of period t are given as follows[25]

$$x_1(t) = \left[\begin{array}{ll} x_2(t), & \text{if the guest–worker remigrates at } t \\ 0, & \text{otherwise} \end{array} \right. \tag{1}$$

Now the actual values of $x_j(t)$ are determined (besides (re)migration decisions) by consumption decisions and – more basically – by a set of realized economic variables, namely:

$p_j(t)$: (strictly positive) price per unit of the (aggregate) consumption good, in country j, during period t

$\Pi(t)$: (non–negative) nominal return on investment in country 1, during period t; i. e. if an amount $x_1(t)$ is invested at the beginning of period t in country 1, then the income $\Pi(t)x_1(t)$ is obtained during period t

$y(t)$: (strictly positive) nominal wage income, in country 2 during period t.

r_j : nominal interest factor (≥ 1) on (dis–)saving in country j.

We assume r_j to be known to the decision maker, whereas the sequence $\{z(t)\}_{t=0}^{T}$ of "data"–vectors

$$z(t) := (\Pi(t), p_1(t), p_2(t), y(t)) \tag{2}$$

is from the migrant's subjective point of view a Markov process with transition probabilities $\varphi_t(\cdot|z(t))$. I. e. the migrant is supposed to be incompletely informed about the data sequence $\{z(t)\}$ at the beginning of the decision process; but he is able to make a probabilistic prediction about $z(t+1)$, if he knows $z(t)$. – Furthermore it is assumed that the migrant knows $z(t)$ at the beginning of period t.

Therefore from $\{z(t)\}_{t=0}^{T}$ we obtain the following dynamics for the sequence $\{x_j(t)\}_{t=0}^{T}$ of assets

$$x_1(t+1) = \left[\begin{array}{ll} r_1\left(\Pi(t)x_1(t) - p_1(t)c(t)\right) & \text{if the migrant lives in country 1} \\ & \text{during period } t \text{ and consumes } c(t) \\ 0, & \text{otherwise} \end{array} \right. \tag{3}$$

[25]Here and in the sequel of this chapter we do not regard explicitly the exchange–rate problem, it is not essential for our purposes (speculative aspects are not considered). All money values may be interpreted as evaluated in the currency of country 1.

$$x_2(t+1) = \begin{cases} r_2\,(x_2(t) + y(t) - p_2(t)c(t)) & \text{if the migrant lives in country 2 during period } t \text{ and consumes } c(t) \\ 0, & \text{otherwise} \end{cases} \tag{4}$$

with $x_1(0) = x_2(0) = 0$.

The final ingredients of our model are a sequence $\{u_t\}_{t=1}^{T}$ of per–period utility functions $u_t : \mathbf{R} \to \overline{\mathbf{R}}$ representing the migrant's preferences on the set of consumption streams $c_t \in \mathbf{R}$. And a final reward function $u_{T+1} : \mathbf{R} \to \overline{\mathbf{R}}$ representing the migrant's preferences on final assets x_{T+1}, and the usual discounting factor $\beta > 0$.

Now we will show how this general Temporary– vs. Permanent–Migration Model can be formalized as a Markovian decision process: a **typical state** at the beginning of period t is given by

$$s(t) = (z(t), x_1(t), x_2(t), j(t)), \tag{5}$$

where $j(t) \in \{1,2\}$ denotes the country where the individual is still living at the beginning of period t, $x_j(t)$ is his asset in country j at the beginning of t and $z(t)$ is the data–vector given by (2). (Thus we adopt here a special "state–of–the–economy" interpretation). The **state space** S can then be written as

$$S := S_1 \cup S_2 \tag{6}$$

with

$$S_j := \bar{Z} \times \bar{X}_1 \times \bar{X}_2 \times \{j\}, \quad \bar{Z} := \mathbf{R}_+ \times \mathbf{R}^3_{++}, \quad \bar{X}_j := R \tag{7}$$

(The order of the components of $z \in \bar{Z}$ should be kept in mind: $z = (\Pi, p_1, p_2, y)$!).

The (in general state–dependent) **action sets** are defined as follows

$$A_t(s) := \begin{cases} \{(c,1); c \in \mathbf{R}\}, & \text{if } \; s \in S_1 \\ \{(c,1); c \in \mathbf{R}\} \cup \{(c,2); c \in \mathbf{R}\}, & \text{if } \; s \in S_2 \end{cases} \quad (t \geq 2) \tag{8}$$

$$A_1(s) := \{(c,j); c \in \mathbf{R}\}, \quad \text{if } \; s \in S_j, \tag{9}$$

$$A_0(s) := \{1,2\}. \tag{10}$$

Furthermore we get the following stochastic non–homogeneous **transition law** $P_t(\cdot|\cdot,\cdot) : B(S) \times S \times A_t \to [0,1]$, where $A_t := \cup_{s \in S} A_t(s)$ for $t \geq 2$:

$$P_t(Z \times X_1 \times X_2 \times \{j\}|s,(c,1)) := \begin{cases} \varphi_t(Z|z) & \text{if } j = 1,\ r_1(\Pi x_1 - p_1 c) \in X_1, \ 0 \in X_2 \\ 0, & \text{otherwise} \end{cases} \tag{11}$$

where $Z \in B(\bar{Z})$, $X_j \in B(\bar{X}_j)$, $s = (z, x_1, x_2, 1) = (\Pi, p_1, p_2, y, x_1, x_2, 1) \in S_1$

$$P_t(Z \times X_1 \times X_2 \times \{j\}|s,(c,2)) := \begin{cases} \varphi_t(Z|z) & \text{if } j = 2,\ r_2(x_2 + y - p_2 c) \in X_2,\ 0 \in X_2 \\ 0, & \text{otherwise} \end{cases} \tag{12}$$

if $s = (z, x_1, x_2, 2) = (\Pi, p_1, p_2, y, x_1, x_2, 2) \in S_2$, and finally for the same $s \in S_2$

$$P_t(Z \times X_1 \times X_2 \times \{j\}|s,(c,1)) := \begin{bmatrix} \varphi_t(Z|z) & \text{if } j = 1,0 \in X_2, \text{ and } \\ & r_1(\Pi(x_1+x_2) - p_1 c) \in X_1, \\ & 0 \in X_2 \\ 0, & \text{otherwise} \end{bmatrix} \tag{13}$$

It should be obvious – despite the tedious notations – that these transition probabilities essentially reflect the asset dynamics (3) and (4), and furthermore the asset–transfer condition (1).

As we assume $s(0) = (z(0), 0, 0, 1) \in S_1$ with some fixed $z(0) \in \bar{Z}$, i. e. essentially that the individual lives at the beginning of the decision process in his home country, and has no assets in both countries, we have to define the transition law $P_0(\cdot|s,j)$ only for $s = s(0)$.

It is given by

$$P_t(Z \times X_1 \times X_2 \times \{j'\}|s,j) := \begin{bmatrix} \varphi_t(Z|z(0)) & \text{if } j = j', \text{ and } 0 \in X_1, \\ & 0 \in X_2, \\ 0, & \text{otherwise} \end{bmatrix} \tag{14}$$

And since only states $s = (z, 0, 0, j) \in S_j$ can be reached at the beginning of period 1, we have to define the transition law only for such states $s \in S_j$ and for actions $(c, j) \in A_1(s)$:

$$P_1(Z \times X_1 \times X_2 \times \{j'\}|s,(c,j)) := \begin{bmatrix} \varphi_t(Z|z(0)) & \text{if } \; s \in S_1, j = j' = 1 \\ & \text{if } \; s \in S_2, j = j' = 2 \\ 0, & \text{otherwise} \end{bmatrix} \tag{15}$$

Assuming zero–(re)migration costs in this model the reward functions $\tilde{u}_t : S \times A_t \rightarrow \mathbf{R}$ are given by[26]

$$\begin{bmatrix} \tilde{u}_0 \equiv 0; & \\ \tilde{u}_t(s,(c,j)) = u_t(c), & t = 1, \ldots, T \\ \tilde{u}_{T+1}(s) = u_{T+1}(x_j) & \text{for } \; s = (z, x_1, x_2, j) \end{bmatrix} \tag{16}$$

Now let us consider a 'strategy' in the context of the temporary– vs. permanent–migration decision process. In period 0 such a strategy must prescribe a migration decision, whereas in the following periods $t \geq 1$, it prescribes – generally – a consumption– and remigration–decision. Formally a strategy here is a sequence $\sigma = (\sigma_0, \sigma_1, \ldots, \sigma_T)$ with $\sigma_t : S \rightarrow A_t$ such that $\sigma_t(s) \in A_t(s)$, $(t = 0, \ldots, T)$. With each strategy there is associated the expected payoff

$$F(\sigma) := E_{P_\sigma}\left[\sum_{t=1}^{T} \beta^t u_t(\sigma_t^c(\cdot)) + \beta^{T+1} u_{T+1}(\cdot)|s(0)\right] \tag{17}$$

[26]Because of our restrictions concerning transfers of assets and migrations it follows that in each terminal state $s = (z, x_1, x_2, j)$ we have $x_k = 0$ for $k \neq j$, i. e. at the end of the planning horizon the migrant has only non–zero assets in the country where he is living then.

where $P\sigma$ is the probability measure on $\bigotimes_{t=1}^{T} B(S)$ induced by σ via the transition probabilities, and σ_t^c denotes the consumption -decision part of the action $\sigma_t(s) = (c_t, j_t)$ prescribed by σ_t. Now let σ^* be an optimal strategy i. e. a strategy such that we have

$$F(\sigma^*) = \sup_{\sigma} F(\sigma).$$

Definition II.2.1: *Migration from country 1 to country 2 will be called* **temporary** *if $\sigma_0^*(s_0) = 2$ and if there is a t, $1 < t \leq T$, such that the action in period t resulting from σ_t^* implies remigration from 2 to 1. If $\sigma_0^*(s0) = 2$ and all actions for all $t = 1, \ldots, T$ resulting from σ_t^* imply staying in country 2, then we will speak of* **permanent migration.**

We are primarily interested in characterizing the set of possible realizations

$$\underline{z} = (z_1, z_2, \ldots, z_T) \in \bar{Z}^T$$

with $z_t = (\Pi_t, p_{1t}, p_{2t}, y_t)$ of the data process $\{z(t)\}_{t=1}^{T}$ leading to the "temporary vs. permanent"-migration phenomenon - as verbally described in section II.1. To do this we proceed as follows. Primarily let us consider the "stopping-time" t^* induced by an optimal strategy σ^* and given by

$$t^*(\underline{z}) := \left[\begin{array}{ll} \min\{t : 2 \leq t \leq sT : \sigma_t^*(z_t, x_{1t}^*, x_{2t}^*, 2) = (c_t^*, 1)\} & \text{if the "min" exists} \\ T+1, & \text{otherwise} \end{array} \right. \tag{18}$$

where the sequences $\{x_{jt}^*\}_{t=1}^{T}$ are inductively defined by

$$\begin{array}{rcl} x_{21}^* & = & 0 \\ x_{2t+1}^* & = & \left[\begin{array}{ll} r_2(x_{2t}^* + y_t - p_{2t}c_t^*), & \text{if} \quad \sigma_t^*(z_t, x_{12}^*, x_{2t}^*, 2) = (c_t^*, 2) \\ 0, & \text{otherwise} \end{array} \right. \end{array} \tag{19}$$

$$\begin{array}{rcl} x_{11}^* & = & 0 \\ x_{2t+1}^* & = & \left[\begin{array}{ll} 0, & \text{if} \quad \sigma_t^*(z_t, x_{1t}^*, x_{2t}^*, 2) = (c_t^*, 2) \\ r_1(\Pi_t x_{2t}^* - p_1 c_t^*), & \text{if} \quad \sigma_t^*(z_t, x_{1t}^*, x_{2t}^*, 2) = (c_t^*, 1) \end{array} \right. \end{array} \tag{20}$$

i. e. the sequences $\{x_{jt}^*\}$ describe the sequences of assets resulting from the strategy σ^*, and applied to the trajectory $\underline{z}$ of the Markov process $\{z(t)\}_{t=1}^{T}$. Then $t^*(\underline{z})$ is the period where the guest-worker remigrates, according to the optimal strategy σ^*, if $\underline{z}$ occurs.

Now let us define the sequence of **remigration sets**

$$R_t := \{\underline{z} \in \bar{Z}^T : t^*(\underline{z}) \leq t\}, \quad (2 \leq t \leq T) \tag{21}$$

i. e. the set of data -, i. e. return on investment-, price-levels-, income-sequences $\underline{z}$ inducing remigration before period t.

We are able to define the "temporary vs. permanent-migration phenomenon" in an unambiguous formal way.

Definition II.2.2:

a) *We will say that a guest–worker "is planning temporary migration of at most* $t < T$ *periods", if there is an initial data constellation* $z_0 = (\Pi_0, p_{10}, p_{20}, y_0)$ *such that*

$$\sigma_0^*(z_0, 0, 0, 1) = 2 \tag{22a}$$

and such that for the expectation of the stopping time t^* *w.r. to the probability* P_φ *on* $\bar{Z}^T$ *induced by the transition probabilities* $\varphi_t(\cdot|\cdot)$

$$E_{P_\varphi}(t^*|z_0) \leq t \tag{22b}$$

holds.

b) *The "temporary vs. permanent-migration phenomenon" occurs, if the guest–worker is planning a temporary migration of at most* $t < T$ *periods, whereas a trajectory* $\underline{z} \in \bar{Z}^T \setminus R_t$ *is realized.*

REMARKS: 1. Instead of (22b) we could postulate:

$$P_\varphi(R_t|z_0) \geq 1 - \epsilon \tag{22b'}$$

for some $\epsilon > 0$.

2. For both (22b) and (22b'), the "temporary vs. permanent –migration phenomenon" is – according to our definition – the result of an "overestimation" of the size of the remigration set R_t by the guest–worker, caused by his incomplete information. – We claim that this definition captures the central idea of this phenomenon as pronounced in verbal terms by empirical researchers on guest–worker migration; (compare the cited works in the introduction to this chapter).

3. In our opinion this definition could also be an appropriate starting point for analyzing the "temporary vs. permanent migration phenomenon" as a mass phenomenon – and not only as an individual "accident". For this it would be necessary to introduce an objective probability measure P' on $\bar{Z}^T$ – as opposed to the subjective probability measure of an individual guest–worker used here, and to compute and to analyse the objective probability $P'(\bar{Z}^T \setminus R_t)$ of the event that a trajectory does not belong to the remigration set R_t. This theme will not be pursued here, but will be the subject of further research in the spirit of this chapter.

In the next section we will study the shape of the remigration set R_2 in the case of $T = 2$ and under additional special assumptions; the rest of the present section is dealing with the description of the sets R_t in more general cases. For this sake we will first characterize an optimal strategy σ^* by the value functions of the decision problem. We define in the usual way for $t = 1, \ldots, T$

$$V_t(s) := \sup_{\sigma(t)} \left\{ E_{P_{\sigma(t)}} \left[\sum_{\tau=t}^{T} \beta^\tau u_\tau(\sigma_\tau^c(\cdot)) + \beta^{T+1} u_{T+1}(\cdot) | s(t) = s \right] \right\} \tag{23}$$

as the maximum expected payoff which can be obtained if the decision process starts in period t in state $s(t) = s$ and strategies $\sigma(t) = (\sigma_t, \ldots, \sigma_T)$ with $\sigma_\tau : S \to A_\tau$ such that $\sigma_{\tau(s)} \in A_{\tau(s)}$ are used. Furthermore let us define

$$V_0(s(0)) := F(\sigma^*) \tag{24}$$

and

$$V_{T+1}(s) := u_{T+1}(x) \tag{25}$$

Since in our decision process the subset S_1 of the state space S is absorbing for $t \geq 1$ (the formal equivalent of the fact that migration from 1 to 2 is only allowed in period 0), for each $t \geq 1$ each state $s(t) = s = (\Pi, p_1, p_2, y, x_1, x_2, 1) \in S_1$ induces an initial state $\hat{s}_1 = (\Pi, p_1, x_1) \in \hat{S}_1$ of a $(T-t)$-stage decision process with state space $\hat{S}_1$, with action sets $A_\tau = \{c; c \in R\}$ and transition probabilities given by relations similar to (15) and (13). Let $\hat{V}_t(s_1)$ denote the value of this **consumption–decision process in country 1.**

This leads to the following form of the optimality equations for the temporary– vs. permanent–migration–decision process: (for $t \geq 1$):

$$\hat{V}_t(s) = \hat{V}_t(\hat{s}_1) = \sup_c \left\{ u_t(c) + \beta \int \hat{V}_{t+1}(\hat{z}(t+1), r_1(\Pi x_1 - p_1 c)) d\hat{\varphi}_t(\hat{z}(t+1)|\hat{z}) \right\} \tag{26}$$

and

$$\begin{aligned} V_t(s) \quad = \quad & \max \Big[\hat{V}_t(\hat{s}_1), \sup_c \{ u_t(c) \\ & + \beta \int V_{t+1}(z(t+1), x_1, r_2(x_2 + y - p_2 c), 2) d\varphi_t(z(t+1)|z) \} \Big] \end{aligned} \tag{27}$$

(here $\hat{\varphi}_t$ denotes the transition probability (induced by φ_t) for the subprocess $\{\hat{z}(t)\}_{t=1}^T$ of $\{z(t)\}_{t=1}^T$ with

$$\hat{z}(t) = (\Pi(t), p_1(t)) \quad \text{for} \quad z(t) = (\Pi(t), p_1(t), p_2(t), y(t))).$$

The first relation says that the value of the temp.– vs. perm. –migration decision process, if remigration already took place or if no migration took place, is equal to the value of the consumption decision subprocess in country 1.

The second relation shows that the value of the decision process, starting from a state in country 2, is the maximum of the value of the consumption–decision process starting from the same state unless the guest–worker has remigrated, and of the best payoff which can be obtained by staying in country 2 for at least one period consuming and working there, and thus retaining the option to remigrate one period later.

Furthermore the value $V_0(s(0))$ can be written as

$$V_0(s(0)) = \beta \max \left\{ \int \hat{V}_1(\hat{z}(1), 0, 1) d\hat{\varphi}_0(\hat{z}(1)|\hat{z}(0)), \int V_1(z(1), 0, 2) d\varphi_0(z(1)|z(0)) \right\} \tag{28}$$

since u_0 was assumed to equal zero.

Using these forms of the optimality equations we may characterize the remigration sets.

Proposition II.2.1: *The remigration sets R_t, defined in (21), may be written as*[27]

$$R_t = \{\underline{z} \in \bar{Z}^T | \hat{V}_t(\hat{z}_t, x^*_{2t}) = V_t(z_t, 0, x^*_{2t}, 2)\} \tag{29}$$

In other words, remigration will take place exactly in period t for such $\underline{z}$ where

$$\hat{V}_\tau(z_\tau, x^*_{2\tau}) < V_\tau(z_\tau, 0, x^*_{2\tau}, 2) \quad \textit{for} \quad \tau = 2, \ldots, t-1$$

and

$$\hat{V}_t(\hat{z}_t, x^*_{2t}) = V_t(z_t, 0, x^*_{2t}, 2).$$

Obviously it would be rather difficult to derive some interesting testable implications from our model at the current level of generality. Therefore we will specialize the general framework by restricting the analysis to an essentially 2–period model.[28]

II.3 Analysis of the Remigration Set for $T = 2$

In the introduction we have mentioned some reasons which could in reality prevent the target–saving guest–worker from hitting his target within the planned period. Among others there are: higher prices and lower incomes in the host country, coupled with higher prices and lower return on investment in the home country. Therefore a possible empirical test of our temporary– vs. permanent–migration–decision model would be to examine whether this model in the case of $T = 2$ is able to predict:

(P) *For fixed real Π_2/p_{12} and for fixed p_{22} and y_2, remigration in period t becomes less probable the higher p_{21} and the smaller y_1.*

For such a 'prediction' would mean that unfavourable saving conditions in the guest-country 2 induce a delay of remigration.

Obviously this prediction is in sharp contrast to a hypothesis derived from a MAB–model of international migration. According to the latter model, high p_{21} and small y_1 would be "bad" conditions in the host country leading to a higher probability of remigration.

It is the aim of this section to show that (P) can be derived from the temporary– vs. permanent–migration model under special assumptions. For this sake we will analyse the remigration set R_2 in more detail.

According to Proposition II.2, together with formulas (26) and (27) in II.2, we obtain: The trajectory $(z_1, z_2) = (\Pi_1, p_{11}, p_{21}, y_1, \Pi_2, p_{12}, p_{22}, y_2)$ belongs to the remigration set R_2 iff

$$\max_c\{u_2(c) + \beta u_3(r_1(\Pi_2 x^*_{22} - p_{12}c))\} \geq \max_c\{u_2(c) + \beta u_3(r_2(x^*_{22} + y_2 - p_{22}c))\}. \tag{30}$$

[27] Here we adopt the tie–breaking rule: "remigration to 1" in the case of indifference.

[28] The following section relies heavily on Berninghaus/Seifert–Vogt (1988).

It should be remarked that z_1 influences this inequality via the asset x^*_{22} (compare (19)):

If we assume

$$u_3(x) = \begin{cases} 0, & \text{for} \quad x \geq 0 \\ -\infty, & x < 0 \end{cases} \tag{31}$$

$$u_2 \quad \text{stricly increasing,} \tag{32}$$

then (30) specializes to

$$\eta x^*_{22} \geq x^*_{22} + y_2 \tag{33}$$

with the abbreviation:

$$\eta := (p_{22}/p_{12})\Pi_2. \tag{34}$$

Because of $x^*_{21} = 0$ and $x^*_{22} = r_2(y_1 - p_{21}c^*_1)$, where c^*_1 is the optimal consumption decision in country 2 in period 1 – compare again formula (19) in II.2 – (33) is equivalent to

$$\eta r_2(y_1 - qc^*_1) \geq r_2(y_1 - qc^*_1) + y_2 \tag{35}$$

with the additional abbreviation

$$q := p_{21}. \tag{36}$$

Thus instead of analyzing the shape of r_2 we are led to examine whether the **(reparametrized) remigration set**

$$R^*_2 := \{(\eta, y_2, q, y_1) \in \mathbf{R}_+ \times \mathbf{R}^3_{++} | \text{for} \quad \eta, q, y_1 \quad \text{and} \quad y_2 \quad \text{holds} \quad (35)\} \tag{37}$$

has a particular shape which would allow the prediction (P).

Unfortunately this does not seem to be possible without some restrictive assumptions concerning the utility functions u_t and transition probabilities $\varphi(\cdot|\cdot)$. The following list of assumptions will turn out to be appropriate. Some comments concerning these assumptions will be given at the end of this section.

(A.1)

The per–period utility functions u_t are given by

$$u_1(c_1) := \begin{cases} \ln(c_1 - b), & c_1 > b \\ -\infty, & \text{otherwise} \end{cases}$$

with some $b > 0$

$$u_2(c_2) := \begin{cases} \ln c_2, & c_2 > 0 \\ -\infty, & \text{otherwise} \end{cases}$$

$$u_3(x) := \begin{cases} 0, & x \geq 0 \\ -\infty, & \text{otherwise} \end{cases}$$

(A.2)

The stochastic "process" $\{z(1), z(2)\}$ with $z(t) = (\eta(t), p_1(t), p_2(t), y(t))$ and the transition probabilities φ_t obey the following conditions:

a) The marginal distributions of $y(1)$ and $y(2)$ are degenerated at fixed values y_1 and y_2.

b) The random vector $(\Pi(2), p_1(2), p_2(2))$ is stochastically independent of the random vector $(\Pi(1), p_1(1), p_2(1))$.

c) The random variable $\tilde{\eta} := (p_2(2)/p_1(2))\Pi(2)$ is Pareto–distributed with cumulative distribution function

$$H(\eta) := \left[\begin{array}{ll} 0, & \text{for} \quad \eta \leq 1 \\ 1 - 1/\eta, & \text{for} \quad \eta > 1 \end{array} \right.$$

(A.3)

$$r_2 y_1 > y_2$$

Then we can formulate the main result of this section in the proposition below:

Proposition II.3.1: *Suppose assumptions (A.1), (A.2) and (A.3) are fulfilled. Then there exists a price* $q > 0$*, and a function*

$$f : (0, \hat{q}) \to \mathbf{R}_+$$

where $f(\cdot)$ *is (i) strictly increasing, (ii) strictly convex and (iii) bounded below by 1, such that the* (y_1, y_2)*–section* $R_2^*(y_1, y_2)$ *of the reparametrized remigration set* R_2^* [29] *can be written as follows:*

$$R_2^*(y_1, y_2) = \{(\eta, q) \in \mathbf{R}_+ \times \mathbf{R}_{++} | q \in (0, \hat{q}) \quad \textit{and} \quad \eta \geq f(q)\}.$$

The proof of the proposition is rather lengthy and tedious; it is given in the appendix. There it is also demonstrated that $f(\cdot)$ can be chosen to be equal to

$$f(q) = 1 + y_2/x_2^*(q)$$

with $x_2^*(q) = r_2(y_1 - qc_1^*(q))$ the return at the beginning of period 2 from saved income $(y_1 - qc_1^*(q))$ from period 1. Consequently $x_2^*(q)f(q)$ can be interpreted as the maximum expenditure for the guest–worker if he stays in the home–country 2 until the end of the planning horizon. Therefore $f(q)$ is the maximum expenditure for period 2 in country 2 per unit of saved money during the first period in 2. And the remigration decision ($\eta \geq f(q)$ rsp. $\Pi_2/p_{12} \geq f(q)/p_{22} = f(p_{21})/p_{22}$) is based on comparing the real return on investment in the home country and the real maximum consumption per unit of money gained by saving in period 1 in host country 2. Obviously we can illustrate the result of Proposition II.3.1 by the following drawing

[29] The (y_1, y_2)–section of R_2^* is defined as:

$$\begin{aligned} R_2^*(y_1, y_2) &:= \{(\eta, q) \in \mathbf{R}_+ \times \mathbf{R}_{++} | (\eta, y_2, q, y_1) \in \mathbf{R}_2^*\} \\ &= \{(\eta, q) \in \mathbf{R}_+ \times \mathbf{R}_{++} | \text{for} \quad (\eta, y_2, q, y_1) \quad \text{holds (35)}\}. \end{aligned}$$

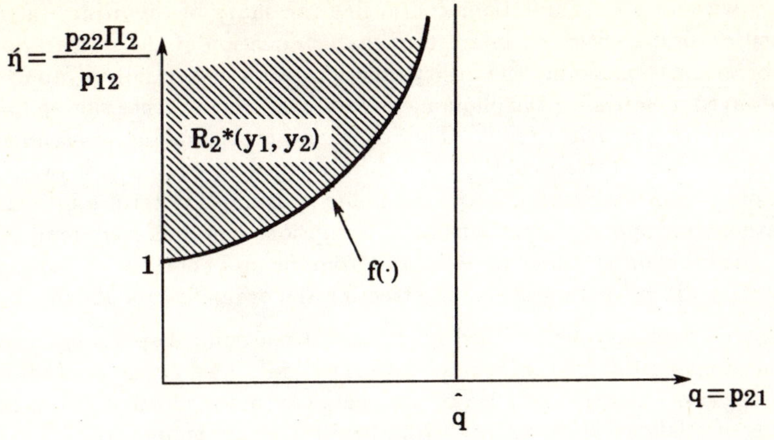

Figure 8: Illustration of the remigration set R_2^*

As can be seen from the figure, for fixed real Π_2/p_{12} and for fixed p_{22} and y_2 and y_1, remigration in the second period $t = 2$ becomes the less probable the higher p_{21}. And there exists a critical price–level $\hat{q}$ for p_{21} such that the guest–worker will not remigrate, independent of the profit–opportunities in the home–country, if period–1 price p_{21} is above $\hat{q}$.

Therefore the special assumptions for our temporary– vs. permanent–migration model allow us to derive one essential part of the desired prediction (P). An increasing price p_{21} prevents the guest–worker from saving so much that it is not worthwhile for him to invest the money–asset in his home country.

In considering the effects of variations in the incomes y_1 and y_2 on the remigration decision we have to remember that the optimal first period expenditure $p_{21}c_1^*(p_{21})$ which depends on y_1 and y_2 is a crucial part of the function $f(\cdot)$. Therefore $f(\cdot)$ is also dependent on (y_1, y_2), and it can be shown:

Proposition II.3.2: *Suppose the assumptions (A.1)–(A.3) are fulfilled. Then the function $f(\cdot)$ shifts downwards for increasing y_1 and upwards for increasing y_2.*

The proof of this proposition is given in the appendix too. Thus increasing y_1 enlarges the remigration set R_2^* in the way as asserted in (P). Furthermore, as it should be expected, better income opportunities y_2 in country 2 increase the probability of a permanent migration.

Now let us review the assumptions (A.1)–(A.3) that are sufficient to guarantee the result. Obviously without any assumptions concerning the shape of the utility functions u_t and the transition probabilities no interesting characterization of the remigration set R_2 and R_2^* can be given. Concerning the utility functions we use especially u_3 to exclude welfare effects of saved money after the planning horizon and, on the other side to prevent the migrant from ending up with debts. The log–shape of u_1 and u_2 is assumed for computational convenience, (presumably it could be relaxed at the cost of even more tedious calculations). More important is the minimum consumption term b in u_1 which allows to generate intertemporal connections in consumption. One can even demonstrate that the slope of the function $f(\cdot)$ depends on b, and from the proof of lemma 4 (appendix) one can see that $f(\cdot)$ will be a straight line intersecting the ordinate axis at 1 for $b = 0$.

We claim that (A.2)a) may be justified by empirical reasoning Especially in guest–worker migration the potential migrant is more or less well informed about the (nominal!) wage income in the host–country, because of contracts concluded already in the home–country by means of a labour–office agency with a guest–country employer.

Concerning the independence of $\hat{z}(2) := (\Pi(2), p_1(2), p_2(2))$ and $(\Pi(1), p_1(1), p(1))$, we can primarily mention that we actually need the independence of $\hat{z}(2)$ and $p_2(1)$. Hereby the independence of $(\Pi(2), p_1(2))$ from $p_2(1)$ does not seem to be a serious restriction (from an empirical point of view) as both types of variables are generated by economic processes in different countries. Finally the independence of the country–2–prices $p_2(1)$ and $p_2(2)$ should be interpreted in the right way: we do not assert that $p_2(2)$ and $p_2(1)$ actually are stochastically independent, we only suppose that the migrant believes he cannot predict the period–2–price $p_2(2)$ if he knows the period–1–price $p_2(1)$. By assuming the extreme opposite case – the migrant believes $p_2(2)$ to be equal to $p_2(1)$ – we were not able to draw definite conclusions concerning the shape of the remigration set. The reason behind is that the consumption/saving decision in the first period extremely depends on still "enough" uncertainty about $p_2(2)$.

But we believe that it is possible to show that if

$$p_2(2) = p_2^{\alpha}(1)\epsilon$$

with $0 < \alpha < 1$ and a strictly positive random variable ϵ which is independent of $p_2^{\alpha}(1)$, and if the cumulative distribution function of

$$\tilde{\eta} := \epsilon\Pi(2)/p_1(2)$$

(instead of $\eta = p_2(2)\Pi(2)/p_1(2)$) fulfills condition (A.2)c) then the shape of the "remigration–set"

$$R_2^*(y_1, y_2) := \{(\tilde{\eta}, q) \in \mathbf{R}_+ \times \mathbf{R}_{++} | \tilde{\eta} r_2(y_1 - qc_1^*) \geq r_2(y_1 - qc_1^*) + y_2\}$$

can be illustrated by the following drawing:

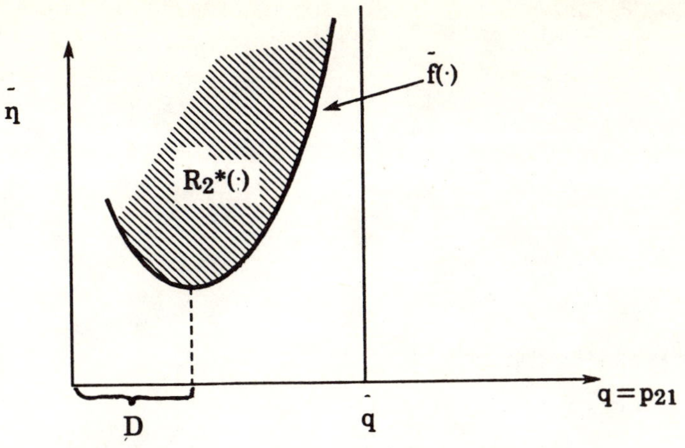

Figure 9: Illustration of the remigration set $R_2^*(\cdot)$

Furthermore it follows that the decreasing part D of $f(\cdot)$ enlarges for increasing α.

Thus even with partial predictability of $p_2(2)$ from $p_2(1)$ – ϵ represents the unpredictable rest – a remigration set $R_2^*(\ldots)$ with at least a part where the "prediction" (P) would hold may be derived from our model.

Concerning the subjective probability distribution over η we assume in (A.2)c) that its cumulative distribution function can be illustrated by the following drawing

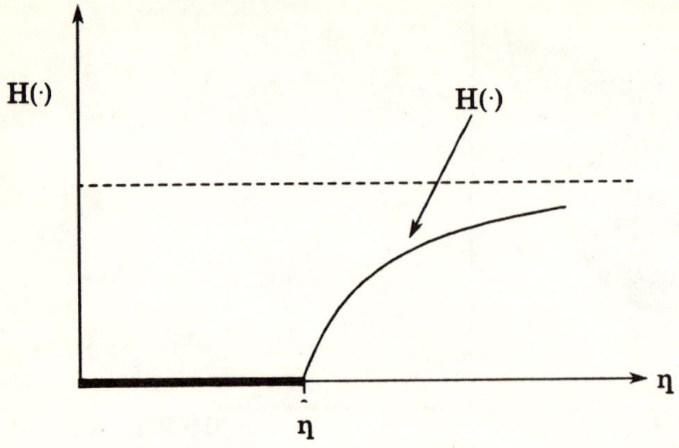

Figure 10: Illustration of $H(\cdot)$

Because of the interpretation of Π_2 it seems to be plausible to suppose that only η values above some positive $\hat{\eta}$ are probable. Indeed our calculations could only be carried through without minor changes, if we supposed H to be of the form

$$H(\eta) := \left[\begin{array}{ll} 0, & \text{for} \quad \eta \leq \hat{\eta} \\ 1 - \hat{\eta}/\eta, & \text{for} \quad \eta > \hat{\eta} \end{array} \right.$$

with some $\hat{\eta} > 0$. Naturally the special functional shape of H is a serious restriction concerning the migrant's beliefs about Π_2, p_{22} and p_{12}; especially it is asserted that the migrant believes values of η near $\hat{\eta}$ to be realized with a higher probability than large η–values. From a computational point of view (A.2)c) implies strict concavity of the value function $V_1(\cdot)$ in dependence on period–1–consumption in the interval $(b, y_1/y_2)$ which simplifies the analysis of the saving/consumption decision considerably. Fortunately, we have been able to show that our results in Propositions II.3.1 and II.3.2 are not too sensitive if (A.2)c) is relaxed: if for the cumulative distribution function $H(\cdot)$ of η there is some Pareto distribution $\hat{H}(\cdot)$ of the form

$$\hat{H}\eta := \left[\begin{array}{ll} 0, & \text{for} \quad \eta \leq \hat{\eta} \\ 1 - \hat{\eta}/\eta, & \eta > \hat{\eta} \end{array} \right.$$

with some suitable $\hat{\eta} > 0$ such that

- H dominates $\hat{H}$ with rsp. to first order stochastic dominance, i. e. $1 - H(\eta) \geq 1 - \hat{H}(\eta)\ \forall \eta$, and

- the density functions H' and $\hat{H}'$ do not differ too much, more precisely

$$H'(\eta) - \hat{H}'(\eta) \leq 1/(\eta - 1)\eta^2 \quad \forall \eta$$

then the conclusions of Propositions II.3.1 and 2 hold too.[30]

Finally assumption (A.3) has been made to guarantee that $\hat{q}$ is strictly positive (see Lemma 2 and 3 in the appendix). For incomes y_1 and y_2 with $r_2 y_1 \leq y_2$ it could happen that $\hat{q} = 0$ and consequently $R_2^*(y_1, y_2) = \emptyset$ which would not be an interesting result for our purpose. It follows from (A.3) that the period 2 income y_2 in country 2 should not be essentially larger than the period 1 income y_1 there. Furthermore Lemma 2 (Appendix) shows that $y_1 2 r_2 < y_2$ implies $R_2^*(y_1, y_2) = \emptyset$. Thus by assuming (A.3) we are on the safe side.

[30]The proof of this statement is available on request.

Chapter III

Temporary Equilibria of Migration

III.1 Introductory Remarks

In contrast to the contents of the previous chapters we will now analyse migration problems in an equilibrium framework. It is intuitively clear that all economic implications concerning aggregate migration behaviour should be based on an underlying equilibrium concept. For let us consider, as a thought experiment, a set of potential migrants who are attracted by a particular country. After a lot of them moved into this country the economic conditions there might change considerably and this might induce the remaining potential migrants no longer to go to this country. To deal with this problem adequately one has to take account not only of migration supply into a country but also of migration demand in a country. Both determine the economic conditions and aggregate immigration streams simultaneously in an equilibrium.

In the following sections we focus on labour force migration, where workers are supposed to supply one unit of labour (inelastic labour supply). Consequently the aggregate supply of migrants from country i to j can be identified with a part of aggregate labour supply in country j. Therefore it is plausible to define **migration equilibrium** as a state where the labour markets in all countries are cleared simultaneously, and all workers are pursuing their optimal migration policies. Insofar our model is not a purely partial equilibrium model as it takes account of the interdependence of labour markets in different countries. But it is no general equilibrium model either as all goods markets for example are left out of consideration. Furthermore we do not intend to model a purely static equilibrium state. We isolate a particular period and are asking for migration equilibrium during this period. But this state depends on the previous state of the economy and the subjective expectations about the future states as well. This kind of equilibrium analysis is known in the literature as "Temporary Equilibrium" analysis (see for example Grandmont (1977)).

More precisely, we will attack the migration equilibrium within a temporary equilibrium framework with overlapping generations (of potential migrants). We suppose that members of each generation live for two periods and that each generation that has died out will be substituted by a new generation of identical individuals. Furthermore in each period there are members of the new born generation ("young agents") and of the generation that has been born one period before ("old agents") in the world economy.[32] Migrants are supposed to decide to which country to supply their labour force in each period such that total expected utility is maximized. In the first period of their lives households are supposed to be incompletely informed about the wage rates and the quality of life they are confronted with during the next period. They build expectations about these variables that are formalized by an exogenously given subjective probability distribution.

To avoid unnecessary complications we introduce the production sector in a rather rudimentary way. More precisely, we suppose that the labour demand function in each country can be derived from the marginal productivity function of a representative firm. As a main result we are able to establish conditions that guarantee the existence of a temporary equilibrium on the labour markets of the countries in a given period (section III.3). To elaborate the role of incomplete information in the theory of migration we are able to demonstrate that even in the case of two identical countries bilateral migration will take place if households are incompletely informed about the relevant data in the foreign country. This is in contrast to well-known results in the theory of International Trade. Furthermore we will analyse the impact of increasing the degree of uncertainty in the (subjective) distributions over the relevant variables on the migration flows. We can show that more uncertainty over the relevant variables in the foreign country might increase the incentives for migration. This surprising result has been derived for the first time within a partial-partial equilibrium framework (see e. g. McCall/McCall (1984)). A detailed discussion of this result can be found in sections I.3 and 4 of this monograph. It is interesting to see that this result remains valid in an equilibrium framework.

Even though migration theory had attracted a lot of economists doing research in migration decision-making or doing empirical work, only few papers are concerned with migration equilibria. Models that are most comparable to our framework have been given by Galor (1986), Kemp/Kondo (1986) or Galor/Stark (1987). All cited authors utilize an overlapping generations framework in a temporary equilibrium setting. But the migrants are supposed to be completely informed about all variables relevant for their decision. And furthermore the authors analyse only steady-state equilibria. These papers mainly differ in the motivation for migration. In Galor/Stark (1987) there are technological differences between countries that induce migration, while in the former papers differences in the time preference rate of the households are the driving force for migration.

In the next chapter we begin with a detailed description of the generation structure of the world economy (III.2.1) and the individual migration decision (III.2.2). It turns out that our models for individual migration decision-making developed in chap. I are in some sense too complicated to be integrated into an equilibrium framework. Therefore in section III.2.2 we present a simplified version of individual decision-making that still captures the essential features of migration under incomplete information.

In III.3.1 we give sufficient conditions for the existence of a temporary equilibrium of migration. That is, we demonstrate that there exists at least one constellation of migration and remigration flows between the countries and a wage profile for both countries such

[32] This is a standard assumption in most models of temporary equilibrium with overlapping generations (Grandmont (1977)).

that supply and demand is balanced in each country's labour market separately. The existence proof follows standard fixed-point arguments. In section III.3.2 we analyse the role of incomplete information as a migration motive. At first we are able to show that in an equilibrium there exist migration streams between countries that can be regarded as identical from an economic point of view. This phenomenon can be explained by the existence of sufficiently many young migrants who subjectively expect a better quality of life in the foreign country. Secondly we demonstrate that "less information" about a country might raise its attractivity for migration even in an equilibrium state.

Finally in III.4 we give some suggestions for further research in this area.

III.2 Description of the Model

III.2.1 The Generation Structure

For the sake of simplicity we consider a two-country model ($i = 1, 2$). The economic agents (the workers) in each country are supposed to live for two periods. Furthermore in each period the generation of agents that just has died out is supposed to be substituted completely and immediately by a new generation.

Let us denote by L_{it} the set of all workers born in country i during period t. It seems natural to assume

- L_{it} and $L_{it'}$ disjoint for $t \neq t'$
- L_{1t} and L_{2t} disjoint

i. e. each worker has his own identity.

As we want to impose an **overlapping generations** structure on our model we assume that in each period t there are living all agents that have been born in the previous period ("old agents") and all agents that have been born in the present period ("young agents"). Consequently the set of all agents in country i in a period t is given by $L_{it-1} \cup L_{it}$ in a self-sufficient state, i. e. if no migration takes place.

In the following we want to identify the agents with real numbers contained in a given interval of the real line. From a most general point of view one should therefore introduce an agent as a triple (x, j, t), where $x \in [a, b]$, $j \in \{1, 2\}$ and $t \in N$. Then a generation born in period t in country can be represented by the set

$$L_{jt} := [a, b] \times \{j\} \times \{t\}.$$

As we assume furthermore that each generation that has died out after 2 periods of living will be substituted by an "identical generation" we have to put this assumption make precisely within our framework as follows: let us consider a generation born at t

$$[a, b] \times \{j\} \times \{t\};$$

then this generation is substituted by an "identical" one in period $t+2$, that means, it is substituted by the generation

$$[a, b] \times \{j\} \times \{t+2\}.$$

In the same sense we have to interprete our assumption that in each period there do exist 2 identical generations (a "young" and an "old" one) in each country simultaneously as follows:

$$\underbrace{([a, b] \times \{j\} \times \{t-1\})}_{\text{"old" generation}} \cup \underbrace{([a, b] \times \{j\} \times \{t\})}_{\text{"young" generation}}.$$

Finally we should mention that later on we will talk sometimes about "identical" generations in different countries, where we mean two generations

$$[a, b] \times \{i\} \times \{t\} \quad \text{and}$$
$$[a, b] \times \{j\} \times \{t\} \quad (i \neq j).$$

But for ease of notation we will omit in the following this rather messy characterization of generations and simply characterize a generation by an interval $[\cdot]$ contained in the real line and we will characterize an agent in a generation as a real number contained in $[\cdot]$. Then "identity" between generations born in different countries or at different periods will simply be interpreted as identity of intervals $[\cdot]$ of real numbers. The reader will easily infer from the context to which generation a particular migrant belongs.

We are concentrating on each agent as a worker supplying a given unit of labour (inelastic labour supply) and we are disregarding in this chapter the consumption decisions of an agent.

The decision problem each agent has to solve in our model is where to supply his labour force in each period. This is equivalent to the solution of the individual migration problem that will be discussed precisely in the following subsection.

III.2.2 The Individual Migration Decision

We already discussed the individual migration problem as a dynamic decision problem under incomplete information in the first two chapters of this monograph. But the general formal framework that has been introduced before is far too general to be utilized as the decision theoretical foundation for a manageable model of migration equilibrium.

Therefore we will have to simplify the individual decision problem appropriately. This will be done in the present section in a manner that has to preserve the essential characteristics of our general decision problem. That is, we should presumably take account of the incomplete information aspect and furthermore allow revisions of a migration decision later on.

More precisely, we consider the following framework for the migration decision:

- A potential migrant who is living for two periods can only move into the foreign country in the first living period.[33] After having moved into the foreign country the agent decides to stay there or to remigrate into his home country in the last living period.

- Let us consider for example a potential migrant in country 1 at the beginning of period t. Then the following variables are supposed to be relevant for the migration decision.

a) The wage profile

$$(w_t, w_{t+1}) = ((w_{1t}, w_{2t}), (w_{1t+1}, w_{2t+1})) \in \mathbf{R}^4_+$$

where w_{it} denotes the wage rate prevailing in country i in period t.

b) The quality of life in country 2 in period $t+1$

$$x_{2t+1} \in \mathbf{R}$$

which is supposed to be representable by a real number (see also section I.2 of this monograph). Similarly to our reasoning in chapter I we regard this non–pecuniary variable as a corrective for the pecuniary variable w_{2t+1} such that a potential migrant is interested in the total benefit $(w_{2t+1} + x_{2t+1})$. In contrast to our general model in chapter I we model here the quality of life explicitly only for the foreign country (here country 2). Consequently x_{2t+1} could be interpreted for example as the net gain in the quality of life induced by moving from country 1 into country 2.

Without any difficulties we could introduce here migration and/or remigration costs as potential variables relevant for the migration decision. For the sake of simplicity we omit these variables here; but compare Berninghaus/Seifert–Vogt (1989).

The potential migrant in question is supposed to be incompletely informed about the future wage rates in both countries w_{t+1} and the quality of life in country 2 x_{2t+1}. Furthermore he is supposed to have an a priori estimation of the realization of these variables which is technically given by an **expectation function** $\varphi : \mathbf{R}^2_+ \rightarrow M(\mathbf{R}^2_+ \times X)$[34] where $X \subset \mathbf{R}$ denotes the set of possible realizations of the quality of life in country 2. Then $\varphi(\underline{w}_t)$ is the subjective probability measure of the agent about $\underline{w}_{t+1}$ and x_{2t+1}, based on the observation of $\underline{w}_t$.

By this assumption we want to capture the idea that a potential migrant born at the beginning of period t might base his forecasts concerning the vector $(\underline{w}_{t+1}, x_{2t+1})$ on the wage rates at time t $\underline{w}_t$ about which the agent is supposed to be completely informed.

We can illustrate a potential migrant's decision problem by the decision tree in the drawing below.

[33]This could be motivated by legal immigration restrictions.

[34]$M(\mathbf{R}^2_+ \times X)$ denotes the set of all probability measures on the Borel–σ–field $B(\mathbf{R}^2_+ \times X)$.

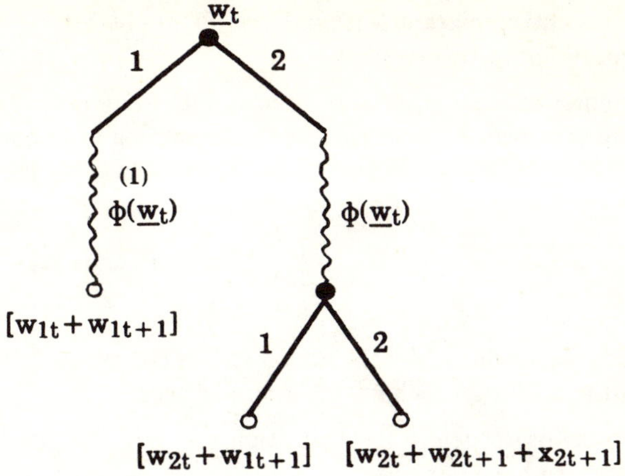

Figure11: A potential migrant's decision tree

Here the numbers at the branches of the decision tree denote the countries the agent (born in country 1) can choose for living in period t and $(t+1)$. $\varphi^{(1)}(\underline{w}_t)$ denotes the marginal probability distribution derived from $\varphi(\underline{w}_t)$ which is a forecast about the wage rate w_{1t+1} only. This corresponds to our assumption that a potential migrant (born in country 1) who has chosen to stay in his home country in the first period of his life is not allowed to move to country 2 in the second period of his life. Finally by the symbol "ξ" we want to symbolize our assumption that $\underline{w}_{t+1}$ and x_{2t+1} are regarded as the realization of random variables.

Before we switch to the solution of this decision problem let us briefly indicate how this particular individual migration problem fits into our general framework of a decision process (see section I.2). Here we have a non–stationary problem where the state and action spaces have a more complicated structure than we need elsewhere in the book. The state spaces are time dependent. Therefore we have for an individual born at the beginning of period t in country 1

$$S_t \subset \mathbf{R}_+^2, S_{t+1} = S_{t+1}^{(1)} \cup S_{t+1}^{(2)} \tag{1}$$

$$\text{where} \quad S_{t+2}^{(1)} \subset \mathbf{R}_+ \quad \text{and} \quad S_{t+1}^{(2)} \subset \mathbf{R}_+ \times X$$

with typical elements $s(t) = (w_{1t}, w_{2t})$ resp. $s(t+1) = w_{1t+1}$ or $s(t+1) =$ $(w_{1t+1}, w_{2t+1}, x_{2t+1})$. Concerning the wages we intend the "state of the economy"–interpretation of the state spaces. That is, the states may change from one period to the next, concerning the quality of life we intend the "state of information"–interpretation of the states. The potential migrant learns about the quality of life in country 2 perfectly after one period of living in this country.

The action spaces are also time– and additionally state–dependent, in the following way (for an agent born in country 1 at the beginning of period t)

$$A_t = \{1,2\}$$

$$A_{t+1}(s) = \left[\begin{array}{ll} \{1\}, & \text{if} \quad s \in S^{(1)}_{t+1} \\ \{1,2\}, & \text{if} \quad s \in S^{(2)}_{t+1} \end{array} \right. \tag{2}$$

This particular definition of the action spaces corresponds to our particular restrictions imposed on the migration behaviour of an old agent.

Now it remains to define the transition law and the reward function $u(\cdot)$. Starting with the latter we have obviously

$$\begin{array}{rl} u(s(t),1) := w_{1t}, & u(s(t),2) := w_{2t}, \\ u(s(t+1),1) = w_{1t+1}, & u(s(t+1),2) = w_{2t+1} + x_{2t+1}. \end{array} \tag{3}$$

Concerning the transition probability we can define for $s(t) = \underline{w}_t$

$$\begin{array}{rl} P(B_1|s(t),1) := \varphi(1)(\underline{w}_t)(B_1), & B_1 \in B(\mathbf{R}_+) \\ P(B|s(t),2) := \varphi(\underline{w}_t)(B), & B \in B(\mathbf{R}^2_+ \times X) \end{array} \tag{4}$$

This is not a MAB problem, and if it is considered to be extended over more than two periods it is even no Markovian decision problem (because of the history–dependence of the concepts). To solve this migration problem we therefore have to apply the general "backward solution" method that is utilized in general non–stationary dynamic optimization problems with a finite planning horizon.

That is, in our framework we have to solve the remigration problem first and afterwards we shall solve the migration problem at the beginning of period t.

Now let us consider an agent from country 1 who moved to country 2 in the first period of his life. At the beginning of period $(t+1)$ the migrant exactly knows $(\underline{w}_{t+1}, x_{2t+1})$ and obviously he will remigrate **iff** the inequality[35]

$$D_1(\underline{w}_{t+1}, x_{2t+1}) := [w_{1t+1} - (w_{2t+1} + x_{2t+1})] > 0 \tag{5}$$

is satisfied. $D_1(\cdot)$ can be interpreted as the net benefit from remigration. Naturally, a migrant will return to his home country if this benefit is positive and he will stay for the rest of his life in the host country if this benefit is negative.

In solving the migration problem of a young agent in country 1 born at t we presuppose that the remigration problem in the following period $t+1$ would be solved optimally in the case of migrating to country 2 during period t. I.e. knowing the realized values $(\underline{w}_{t+1}, x_{2t+1})$ the agent would then solve the problem $\max\{w_{2t+1} + x_{2t+1}, w_{1t+1}\}$. Taken

[35]Implicitly we apply the tiebreaking rule that the migrant will stay in country 2 if $D_1(\cdot) = 0$.

this for granted we may state an analogous inequality as above for describing the migration behaviour. A young agent born in country 1 in period t and characterized by his expectation function φ will migrate to country 2 iff[36]

$$E_1(\underline{w}_t, \varphi) > 0 \tag{6}$$

where $E_1(\cdot,\cdot)$ is given by

$$\begin{aligned} E_1(\underline{w}_t, \varphi) &:= w_{2t} + \int \max\{w_{2t+1} + x_{2t+1}, w_{1t+1}) d\varphi(\underline{w}_t)(\underline{w}_{t+1}, x_{2t+1}) \\ &\quad - w_{1t} - \int w_{1t+1} d\varphi^{(1)}(\underline{w}_t)(w_{1t+1}) \\ &= w_{2t} - w_{1t} + \int [w_{2t+1} + x_{2t+1} - w_{1t+1}]^+ d\varphi(\underline{w}_t)(\underline{w}_{t+1}, x_{2t+1}) \end{aligned} \tag{7}$$

It is obvious from the reasoning above that later on the decision problem allows revision of the migration decision that has already been taken account of at the beginning of the planning horizon. The actual remigration decision will then be based on the information gathered at the beginning of the second living period of the agent. Naturally, in case the inequality

$$E_1(\underline{w}_t, \varphi) \leq 0 \tag{8}$$

is valid the agent need not consider remigration at all.

III.3 Temporary Equilibria of Migration

Obviously from the framework developed in the previous chapter one can derive a labour supply curve for each country generated by the aggregate individual migration decisions. By confronting them with the aggregate labour demand in each country we will derive conditions that guarantee the existence of migration equilibria. Afterwards we will elaborate some characteristic properties of these equilibria.

III.3.1 Definition and Existence of Migration Equilibria

In building up aggregate labour supply from the individual migration decisions in a satisfactory formal way we need some more concepts and some technical assumptions.

At first we suppose:

(A.1) All sets of agents L_{it} are intervals[37] in $\mathbf{R}$, such that the "size" of the set of agents born during period t in country i can be described by the Lebesgue measure $n_{it} := \lambda(L_{it})$.

[36]Here we use the tiebreaking rule that an agent will not migrate if $E_1(\cdot,\cdot) = 0$.

[37]Here the reader should compare our explanations in III.2.1.

The real numbers $n_{it} = \lambda(L_{it})$ should not be confused with the number of agents of a generation, which is clearly infinite in our model.

This "continuum–of–agents"–assumption seems to be a reasonable approximation to large worker sectors in real world economies, and seems to be appropriate for the study of mass phenomena like aggregate migration. From a technical point of view this assumption will turn out as a convenient simplification of our arguments concerning the existence of migration equilibria.

Furthermore we suppose that different agents $l_i \in L_{it}$ may have different expectation functions $\varphi(l_i)$. That is, we postulate

(A.2) There exists a function $\varphi_i(\cdot) : L_{it} \rightarrow \{\varphi | \varphi : \mathbf{R}^2_+ \rightarrow M(\mathbf{R}^2_+ \times X)\}$ such that $\varphi_i(l_i)$ describes the expectation function of agent $l_i \in L_{it}$.

Concerning the quality of life in country j for individuals $l_i \in L_{it-1}$ we suppose that it is the result of a real random experiment that takes place in each period. More precisely, we postulate the existence of a stochastic process

$$X_{jt} : L_{it-1} \times \Omega \rightarrow X \tag{9}$$

that represents the quality of life experiment revealed to the agents $l \in L_{it-1}$ in period t. Let us consider a particular outcome $\omega \in \Omega$ of this random experiment then the function

$$x_{jt}(\cdot) := X_{jt}(\cdot, \omega) : L_{it-1} \rightarrow X \tag{10}$$

is a mapping that associates to each agent $l_i \in L_{it-1}$ the realized value $x_{jt}(l_i)$ of the quality of life he will experience in the foreign country in his second living period. Obviously by $x_{jt}(\cdot)$ we may get more information than is really needed, as in general not all inhabitants of a country will move into the foreign country. Consequently we do not need to know the quality of life of all agents $l_i \in L_{it-1}$. But for technical reasons it seems to be simpler to work with redundant information here.

We do not really utilize the stochastics given by the stochastic process $X_{jt}(\cdot)$ explicitly in the present work. But it seems to be an important starting point for natural extensions of our model that we plan to publish elsewhere. For this sake consider the probability distribution μ_{jt} generated by $X_{jt}(\cdot)$ on the space $(X)^{L_i}$, the space of all quality of life configurations for an economy. Now one could make several hypotheses concerning the evolution of probability measures μ_{jt} over all quality of life configurations in time. The simplest one would be the assumption that μ_{it} does not change at all. Or one could assume steadily "improving" quality of life distributions, where first of all we have to state precisely what we mean by an "improving" process in our particular formal framework. Anyway it will be shown later that a given evolution of $\{\mu_{it}, \mu_{jt}\}_t$ will induce an associated stochastic process of temporary equilibria and consequently would enable us to deal with problems in a more dynamic framework.

Given these concepts, we are able to define migration and remigration streams in each period as follows. Let $M_{it}(\cdot)$ denote the size of the migration stream of young agents from country i into j in period t, and $R_{it+1}(\cdot)$ the size of the stream of old agents (born in country i) remigrating from country j into country i in period $(t+1)$, then we have[38]

$$M_{it}(\underline{w}_t) := \lambda(\{l_i \in L_{it} | E_i(\underline{w}_t, \varphi_i(l_i)) > 0\} \tag{11}$$

$$\begin{aligned} R_{it+1}(\underline{w}_t, x_{jt+1}(\cdot), \underline{w}_{t+1}) \ := \ & \lambda(\{l_i \in L_{it} | E_i(\underline{w}_t, \varphi_i(l_i)) > 0 \\ & \text{and} \quad D_i(\underline{w}_{t+1}, x_{jt+1}(l_i)) > 0\}). \end{aligned} \tag{12}$$

And the size of total labour supply in country i at period t is then given by the following definition[39]

$$\begin{aligned} S_{it}(\underline{w}_{t-1}, \underline{x}_t(\cdot), \underline{w}_t) \ := \ & [n_{it-1} - M_{it-1}(\underline{w}_{t-1})] + \\ & + M_{jt-1}(\underline{w}_{t-1}) + [n_{it} - M_{it}(\underline{w}_t)] + M_{jt}(\underline{w}_t) + \\ & + R_{it}(\underline{w}_{t-1}, x_{jt}(\cdot), \underline{w}_t) - R_{jt}(\underline{w}_{t-1}, x_{it}(\cdot), \underline{w}_t). \end{aligned} \tag{13}$$

According to this definition labour supply in country i is composed of 1) the young agents born in country i who remain in the home country, 2) the young agents from country j who migrate into country i, 3) the old agents, born in country i, who return to country i after having lived for one period in country j, 4) the old agents, born in country j, who migrated into country i in the previous period and do not return to country j, and of 5) the old agents, born in country i, who did not migrate in the previous period and therefore have to stay in country i for the second period of their lives.

We focus in the present monograph on the supply side of the labour market. The demand side will be represented simply by a labour demand function that is the inverse function of a marginal productivity function in country i

$$f_i(\cdot) : \mathbf{R}_+ \to \mathbf{R}_+. \tag{14}$$

By $f_i(\cdot)$, to each value of labour supply s_i in country i there is associated the wage rate $f_i(s_i) = w_i$ that equals marginal productivity of production and consequently is a necessary condition for profit maximization in the firms' sector. Obviously the inverse function $f_i^{-1}(\cdot)$ can be regarded as the labour demand function. We have to admit that this procedure is not very satisfactory from the viewpoint of a rigorous micro–foundation for the aggregate labour demand. But as we are concentrating on worker migration in this monograph we think it can be justified to represent the demand side by the simplest possible model.[40]

Now we are ready to define temporary migration equilibria. We focus on a given period and want to find wage rates w_t^* such that labour supply (including migration streams) and

[38]To guarantee that these definitions are meaningful, some technical assumptions concerning measurability and continuity are needed; compare (A.3) below.

[39]The definition of $S_{jt}(\cdot)$ is analogous.

[40]The demand function can be interpreted as resulting from the solution of the profit maximization problem under perfect competition of a representative firm.

demand equalizes in each country separately. From the wage profile it is then possible to determine the actual equilibrium migration and remigration rates for each country. As the migration decisions in a given period depend partly on the subjectively expected wages in the following period and the remigration rates depend on the wages in the previous periods, we see that the economic activity in each period is somehow linked to the activity in the "neighbouring"-periods. Consequently our model has a similar structure as the well known temporary equilibrium models by Grandmont (1977). As we only consider the labour market we should call our framework a partial temporary equilibrium model. The precise definition is given immediately.

Def. III.3.1: *Let there be given $\underline{w}_{t-1}, \underline{x}_t(\cdot)$, then $\underline{w}_t^* \in \mathbf{R}_+^2$ is called a temporary migration equilibrium in period t iff the following equations are simultaneously satisfied*

$$f_1(S_{1t}(\underline{w}_{t-1}, \underline{x}_t(\cdot), \underline{w}_t^*)) = w_{1t}^*, \tag{15a}$$

$$f_2(S_{2t}(\underline{w}_{t-1}, \underline{x}_t(\cdot), \underline{w}_t^*)) = w_{2t}^*. \tag{15b}$$

It is typical of our equilibrium concept that wage rates are determined in each country's labour market separately but that labour supply is flexible enough to move from one country to the other such that demand and supply will be equilibrated in each country's labour market.

Furthermore it follows from definition 1 that we do not take account of rationing effects in the labour market. Consequently we only consider full employment equilibria in both countries. This seems to make sense in our framework as we do not model the consumption sector, what makes it rather difficult to talk about rationed labour demand in a general equilibrium framework.

As a consistency test for our definition it remains to demonstrate the existence of a migration equilibrium. For this sake we need some technical assumptions about the concepts introduced so far.

At first we will specialize the expectation functions of the agents: we call an expectation function $\varphi : \mathbf{R}_+^2 \to M(\mathbf{R}_+^2 \times X)$ **admissible** if it satisfies the following two conditions:

(i) for each $\underline{w}_t \in \mathbf{R}_+^2$ there is a compact subset $K(\underline{w}_t)$ of $\mathbf{R}_+^2$ containing $\underline{w}_t$ such that the support of $\varphi(\underline{w}_t)$ is contained in $K(\underline{w}_t) \times X$.

(ii) φ is continuous w.r. to the weak topology[41] on $M(\mathbf{R}_+^2 \times X)$.

Condition (ii) says roughly that the expected values of any bounded continuous function of the (subjective) random variables $(\underline{w}_{t+1}, x_{2t+1})$ vary continuously for changing values of $\underline{w}_t$. Condition (i) is essentially a postulate for the marginal distribution of $\varphi(\underline{w}_t)$ w.r. to the wages $\underline{w}_{t+1}$. It says that for $\underline{w}_{t+1}$ only values not too far from $\underline{w}_t$ should be expected to be realized. This assumption does not seem to be too restrictive as an agent usually will not expect future wages to lie far away from present wages.

[41] I.e. in technical terms: The mappings $\underline{w}_t \to \int h(\underline{w}_{t+1}, x_{2t+1}) d\varphi(\underline{w}_t)(\underline{w}_{t+1}, x_{2t+1})$ are continuous for each bounded continuous function $h : \mathbf{R}_+^2 \times X \to \mathbf{R}$ (compare e.g. Parthasarathy (1967), chap. II.6).

Now let us denote the set of all admissible expectation functions by Φ, then we may state our assumption precisely:

(A.3) a) The image set of the functions $\varphi_i(\cdot)$, as introduced in (A.2) is contained in the set Φ

b) For each $\underline{w}_t \in \mathbf{R}_+^2$ the functions $\varphi_i(\underline{w}_t|\cdot) : L_{it} \to M(\mathbf{R}_+^2 \times X)$ are measurable with respect to the Borel–σ–field on $M(\mathbf{R}_+^2 \times X)$ induced by the weak topology.

c) The function $x_{jt}(\cdot) : L_{it-1} \to X$ is measurable.

Whereas b) and c) are merely technical, assumption (A.3)a) postulates that although the expectation functions of different agents $l_i \in L_{it}$ may be different the range of future wage profiles $\underline{w}_{t+1}$ which the agents regard as probable is the same for all $l_i \in L_{it}$.

Furthermore we still have to assume

(A.4)[42] $\lambda(\{l_i \in L_{it}|E_i(\underline{w}_t, \varphi_i(l_i)) = 0\})$ and

$$\lambda(\{l_i \in L_{it-1}|E_i(\underline{w}_{t-1}, \varphi_i(l_i)) > 0 \quad \text{and} \quad D_i(\underline{w}_t, x_{2t}(l_i)) = 0\}) = 0$$

(A.5) $f_i(\cdot)$ is continuous and strictly decreasing.

(A.5) is the standard assumption on marginal productivity in microeconomics. It can easily be derived from strict concavity of the underlying production function (of the representative firm).

(A.4) is a particular assumption that is needed to show the continuity of the labour supply function. Essentially it is postulated by (A.4) that the set of agents who are indifferent between moving to another country and staying[43] is negligible. In the appendix A.III., part B we give a hint as to how (A.4) could be derived from assumptions concerning the original concepts of the model. Technically spoken, we will have to assure that the set of indifferent agents has no non-empty interior. This implies that the Lebesgue–measure of this set is equal to zero.

Now we are ready to give an existence proof for a temporary migration equilibrium.

Proposition III.3.1: *Suppose assumptions (A.1)-(A.5) are satisfied, and let there be given a wage profile* $\underline{w}_{t-1} \in \mathbf{R}_+^2$ *and the realizations* $\underline{x}_t(\cdot)$ *of the quality of life experiments, then there exists a temporary migration equilibrium* $\underline{w}_t^*$.

Proof: See Appendix A.III., part A.

---

[42]It should be noticed that because of (A.3) b) and c) the sets whose measures are assumed to be zero are Lebesgue-measurable.

[43]To be more precise, this means in our framework that the expected pay–off of both actions is the same.

Remark 1: Obviously it follows from assumption (A.5) that $w_{it}^* > 0$ $(i = 1,2)$, as total labour supply, in each country is (by definition) bounded from above by $(2n_1 + 2n_2)$.

Remark 2: The statement in proposition III.3.1 is a pure existence result. Without further restrictions we are not able to exclude multiple equilibria. But as easily can be seen from the proof of the theorem, two different equilibria $\underline{w}_t'$ and $\underline{w}_t^*$ cannot satisfy the relations[44] $w_{it}' < w_{it}^*$ and $w_{jt}' < w_{jt}^*$ $(i,j = 1,2)$ respectively. Only the inequalities $w_{it}' > w_{it}^*$ and $w_{jt}' < w_{jt}^*$ $(i,j = 1,2; i \neq j)$ are compatible with an equilibrium.

Remark 3: According to the proposition and the previous remark there is given an equilibrium correspondence $EQ(\cdot)$ by

$$EQ(\underline{w}_{t-1}, \underline{x}_t(\cdot)) := \{\underline{w}_t^* \in \mathbf{R}_+^2 | \underline{w}_t^* \text{ is a migration equilibrium}\} \tag{16}$$

where $EQ(\underline{w}_{t-1}, \underline{x}_t(\cdot)) = \emptyset$. Then we could make our considerations concerning the stochastic dynamics of the process of temporary equilibria more precise as follows. Let us suppose that the quality of life experiments generate a probability distribution $\mu_t = (\mu_{1t}, \mu_{2t})$. Then we can talk about a probability distribution of migration equilibria in period t, given $\underline{w}_{t-1}$, by the expression

$$Pr(\{\underline{w}_t^* \in A | \underline{w}_{t-1})\} := \mu_t(\{(x_{1t}(\cdot), x_{2t}(\cdot)) \in (X^{L_1} \times X^{L_2})^2 | e(\underline{w}_{t-1}, \underline{x}_t) \in A\}), \tag{17}$$

where $e(\cdot)$ denotes a measurable selection[45] of the equilibrium correspondence $EQ(\cdot)$. Consequently a given transition law for μ_t induces a stochastic process of equilibrium wages $\underline{w}_t^*$ (for analogous reasoning in the theory of general temporary equilibrium see Grandmont/Hildenbrand (1974), Blume (1979,1982)). As we want to concentrate on different topics in the present analysis we will not pursue this idea here any further, which would also need a lot of additional technical machinery.

After we have demonstrated the existence of at least one temporary migration equilibrium we would be interested in particular properties of the equilibrium. In the following section we want to isolate the effects of incomplete information on migration equilibria by keeping the values of all other parameters constant. Insofar we can speak of a comparative static analysis. As we are considering the variation of equilibrium values this analysis is superior to the comparative static studies that are based on an individual migration decision model. As we know from other branches in economic theory, such conclusions that are drawn from individual decision models might often be misleading.

III.3.2 The Effects of Incomplete Information on Temporary Migration Equilibria

In the present section we will investigate the effects of incomplete information of potential migrants by two cases. At first we will analyze migration streams between two "identical" countries. Secondly we will consider the effects of increasing information on the migration streams between two countries.

[44]For in this case we would obtain $f_1^{-1}(w_1') + f_2^{-1}(w_2') \neq 2n_i + 2n_j$.

[45]A measurable selection $e(\cdot)$ of $EQ(\cdot)$ is defined as a measurable mapping such that $e(\cdot) \in EQ(\cdot)$.

III.3.2.1 Equilibrium Migration between "Identical" Countries

The main purpose of this subsection is to give sufficient conditions such that there will be non–zero migration even between countries that are "identical" in a well defined sense. This result seems to be in sharp contrast with traditional results in the Theory of International Trade. Our result is based exclusively on the existence of incompletely informed "young" agents and of disappointed "old" agents who left their home country hoping to find better conditions for living in the foreign country.

But before discussing our results in detail we have to be more precise on the "identical country"–assumption which is crucial for the following arguments. We have to be very rigorous in this assumption to assure that there is no other source of migration than incomplete information.

Def. III.3.2: *Two countries i and j are called to be "in the same economic situation" in period t if the following conditions are satisfied*[46]

$$w_{it-1} = w_{jt-1}, \tag{18a}$$

$$L_{it-1} = L_{jt-1} \quad and \quad L_{it} = L_{jt} \tag{18b}$$

$$x_{it}(\cdot) \equiv x_{jt}(\cdot) \tag{18c}$$

$$\varphi_i(\cdot|\cdot) \equiv \varphi_j(\cdot|\cdot) \quad with \quad \varphi_i(\underline{w}|l_i) := \varphi_i(l_i)(\underline{w}_i) \tag{18d}$$

$$f_i(\cdot) \equiv f_j(\cdot) \tag{18e}$$

As a first step in proving our main result we characterize below the migration and remigration streams between two "identical countries" in a symmetric wage profile ($w_{it} = w_{jt}$). For this sake we need some more assumptions that specify the incomplete information assumption a little bit further:

(A.6) For $i = 1, 2$ we have for all $\underline{w}_t$:

$$\lambda(\{l_i \in L_{it}| \int \max\{w_{jt+1} + x_{jt+1} - w_{it+1}\} d\varphi_i(\underline{w}_t|l_i)(\underline{w}_{t+1}, x_{jt+1}) > 0\}) > 0 \tag{19}$$

Concerning the interpretation of (A.6) we suppose that the set of potential young migrants whose expected net benefits of migration are positive by pursuing the optimal migration policy in the following period is not negligible. According to the definition of $E_i(\cdot)$ this does not automatically imply that a young agent born in i will move to j as it still depends on the current wage rates prevailing in each country. Roughly it can be said that (A.6) essentially requires that there is a "sufficiently large" set of "optimistic" young potential migrants with respect to their subjective expectations about the net return on migration.

[46]Here one should compare our explanations concerning the assumption of "identical generations" in III.2.1.

Furthermore it should be remarked that assumption (A.6) is formulated originally without any reference to the "identical country" assumption. But in the following preparatory lemma we will demonstrate that assumption (A.6) together with the "identical country" assumption will produce the main prerequisite for the proof of the results of this chapter.

Lemma III.3.1: *Suppose (A.6) is valid and countries i and j are "in the same economic situation" in period t. Then we obtain for a symmetric wage profile* $\underline{w}_t = (w, w)$ *the relations*

$$M_{it}(\underline{w}_t) = M_{jt}(\underline{w}_t) = 0, \quad \textit{and} \tag{20a}$$

$$R_{it}(\underline{w}_{t-1}, x_{jt}(\cdot), \underline{w}_t) = R_{jt}(\underline{w}_{t-1}, x_{it}(\cdot), \underline{w}_t). \tag{20b}$$

Proof: See Appendix A.III., part A.

Obviously we cannot guarantee $R_{it}(\cdot) \neq 0$ without stronger assumptions, as one cannot exclude the case

$$\{l_i \in L_{it-1} | E_i(\underline{w}_{t-1}, \varphi_i(l_i)) > 0\} \cap \{l_{it} \in L_{it-1} | D_i(\underline{w}_t, x_{jt}(l_i)) > 0\} = \emptyset \tag{21}$$

which might happen even in the more general model with non–identical countries.

To summarize we can infer from lemma III.3.1 that in a symmetric wage profile there exist migration and remigration streams between both countries of equal size, where we only can guarantee non–trivial migration of some of the young agents. In this sense we can speak of migration even between "identical countries" that is exclusively induced by incomplete information.

Now it remains to be shown that there exists at least one symmmetric temporary migration equilibrium $\underline{w}_t^* = (w^*, w^*)$.

Proposition III.3.2: *Let there be given* $(\underline{w}_{t-1}, x_t(\cdot))$ *and suppose countries i and j are "in the same economic situation" then there exists exactly one symmetric temporary migration equilibrium* $\underline{w}_t^* = (w^*, w^*) \in \mathbf{R}_{++}^2$.

Proof: See Appendix A.III., part A.

It follows from the proof of the proposition that we only can guarantee the existence of a unique symmetric migration equilibrium. Without any further restrictions one cannot exclude the existence of non–symmetric migration equilibria. By combining the results of lemma III.3.1 and proposition III.3.2 we can summarize the main result of the present subsection. Even in "identical countries" with symmetric equilibrium wage profile there will take place migration (in both directions) that is induced by incomplete information of the potential migrants.

III.3.2.2 The Effects of Increasing Uncertainty

The main purpose of this section is to give a generalization of a comparative static result that has been derived from an individual decision theoretical framework elsewhere in this monograph, to an equilibrium framework. In chap. I.3 we showed that a country becomes more attractive for immigration if the "uncertainty" in the quality of life distribution, measured by the mean preserving spread, increases. This result has been derived from Gittins–index theory in determining the optimal migration policy of an incompletely informed decision maker. Furthermore we demonstrated in this context how the result could be interpreted in the direction of decreasing information. More precisely, if one interprets increasing uncertainty as decreasing information in a well defined sense, then our result implies that decreasing information will increase the attractivity of a region and consequently will induce larger immigration streams on the aggregate level.

In the present section we want to show that this result essentially remains valid in our overlapping generations equilibrium framework. For this sake we have to make some additional technical assumptions that mainly guarantee that we really isolate the effects of increasing uncertainty on the equilibrium migration streams. As an important tool we continue to utilize the "identical country" assumption that has been introduced in the previous subsection. More precisely, we consider two countries which are "identical" with one exception: the expectation of the potential migrants in i about the quality of life experienced in j has a larger mean preserving spread than the expectation of the potential migrants in j about the quality of life experienced in country i. Then we will demonstrate that the aggregate migration stream from i to j will be larger than from j to i. To simplify the following arguments we will make the following technical assumptions.

(A.7) The expectation function of an agent $l_i \in L_{it}$ has the form

$$\varphi_i(\underline{w}_t|l_i) := \delta_{\underline{w}_t} \times v_{l_i}(\cdot) \tag{22}$$

where $\delta_{\underline{w}_t}$ denotes the probability measure that is concentrated on $\underline{w}, v_{l_i}(\cdot)$ is a probability measure on $B(X)$ and the symbol "$\times$" denotes a product measure.

In other words, we suppose that the agents use the wage profile in period t as a perfect predictor of the wage profile in period $(t+1)$, while the expectations of the quality of life in period $(t+1)$ are not conditioned on any observation in period t. By this assumption we are able to isolate even the effects of uncertainty in the wage expectations on migration streams. Naturally, one could produce similar results below by concentrating on the effects of increasing uncertainty in the subjective wage expectation function. But in order to keep our reasoning comparable to the decision theoretical results (see chap. I.3) we preferred to focus on the quality of life expectations.

(A.8)

a) $$\{l_i \in L_{it} | \textstyle\int \max\{x_{jt+1}, 0\} dv_{l_i}(x_{jt+1}) > 0\} \neq \emptyset \tag{23a}$$

b) $$\{l_j \in L_{jt} | \textstyle\int \max\{x_{it+1}, 0\} dv_{l_j}(x_{it+1}) > 0\} \subsetneqq L_{jt} \tag{23b}$$

Assumption (A.8) is mainly needed in the crucial step of the proof of the following Proposition. Let us assume that (A.7) is valid and there is given a wage profile $\underline{w}_t = (w, w)$, then the set in (A.8) a) (resp. b)) can be interpreted[47] as the set of agents l_i with

[47]This follows easily from the definition of $E_i(\cdot)$ and $E_j(\cdot)$.

$E_i(\underline{w}_t, \varphi_i(l_i)) > 0$ (and the set of agents l_j with $E_j(\underline{w}_t, \varphi_j(l_j)) > 0$ resp.). Consequently by[48] (A.8) we postulate that in a symmetric wage profile the set of young agents in country i who will actually move for at least one period to country j is not empty and that the set of young migrants who want to move for at least one period from j to i is not equal to the whole generation. From an economic point of view these assumptions do not seem to be too restrictive. Both assumptions characterize the implications of incomplete information of the young agents. Roughly it can be said that there should neither be "extremely many" nor "extremely few" migrants who will try out the foreign country only because they subjectively expect a net benefit from migration.

Now we are prepared to prove the main result of the present subsection.

Proposition III.3.3: *Suppose the two countries ($i = 1, 2$) are "in the same economic situation" in period t with the only exception that*[49] [50]

$$v_{l_i}(\cdot) >_{\text{MPS}} v_{l_j}(\cdot) \text{ for } l_i = l_j \in L_t := L_{it} = L_{jt} \tag{$*$}$$

then a temporary migration equilibrium $\underline{w}_t^*$ is characterized by the inequalities

$$w_{1t}^* > w_{2t}^*, \quad \text{and} \tag{24a}$$

$$M_{1t}(\underline{w}_t^*) > M_{2t}(\underline{w}_t^*). \tag{24b}$$

Proof: See Appendix A.III., part A.

The result in proposition III.3.3 obviously is the analogous statement on an aggregate level concerning the effects of incomplete information on the optimal individual migration policy (see chapter [I.3], Proposition I.3.4). From the theorem we can conclude that migration streams in equilibrium from one country to another will increase if all agents in the former country display more uncertainty in their expectations of the quality of life gained by migration. As a consequence the equilibrium wage in the former country will be larger.

The proof of our result utilizes some techniques (for mean preserving spreads) that also have been applied in the proof of the decision theoretical framework. However, as it can easily be seen from the proof, our result is not a trivial extension of the decision theoretical result. For in equilibrium the wage rates between the two countries have to be different to be compatible with differing migration streams (from i to j and from j to i). And higher wages in country i (see proposition III.3.3 (1)) have a dampening effect

[48] One can easily derive (A.8)a) from (A.6). But we prefer to repeat this assumption here together with (A.8)b) in a different unified form.

[49] By the symbol "...... $>_{\text{MPS}}$ ..." we mean that the probability measure on the left–hand side has a larger mean preserving spread than the probability measure on the right–hand side.

[50] In the following assumption we roughly require that every agent in L_{1t} has a larger MPS in the quality of life distribution in 2 than the corresponding agent in L_{2t} over the quality of life in 1 in period t. According to our explanations in III.2.1 we could interprete ($*$) more rigorously as follows: as we have "identical" generations in both countries we consider the identity mapping $i : [a, b] \rightarrow [a, b]$ that associates to each young agent in 1 uniquely the corresponding agent in 2. Then we suppose that ($*$) is valid for all such pairs of potential migrants.

on migration from i to j and furthermore make country i more attractive for migration of young agents from j to i. But by the proof of proposition III.3.3 it is demonstrated that these off–setting effects are not large enough to overcompensate the positive effects of increasing uncertainty on aggregate migration streams.

Finally it should be remarked that the "identical country" concept might be a powerful tool to handle further comparative static problems in an equilibrium framework. In principle it is a canonical extension of the traditional comparative static method, where some selected exogenous parameters are varied and the effects on the equilibrium values of the endogenous parameters are analysed. By the "identical country" concept we fix the set of relevant exogenous parameters in question. And by relaxing the "identical country" assumption with respect to some selected exogenous parameters we obtain the desired comparative static results in analysing the realized equilibrium values resulting from the particular parameter constellation of almost identical countries.

III.4 Extensions

Naturally, our approach has to be regarded as a first step in modelling migration equilibria based on decision making under incomplete information. In the present subsection we want to give some hints for further research on our model that seems to be most fruitful. At first one could mention the consumption/saving decisions of potential migrants. In our framework potential migrants are active suppliers of labour force. If potential migrants had to solve an intertemporal consumption and saving problem these households would be active demanders of commodities in the countries they are living in. In this context one could also formulate the problem of temporary migration (see chap. II) in an equilibrium setting. Here a migrant plans a temporary stay in the guest country to save enough money to invest it in the home country after remigration. But an unexpected price movement in the guest country might turn temporary into permanent migration. It is easy to see that this extension would complicate our model considerably as we had to introduce explicitly the commodity supply sector. And in this case one should integrate commodity supply and labour force demand into a really General Equilibrium model that could exhibit all the features that have already been derived for temporary equilibrium models of a similar type (see e.g. Grandmont (1977)).

Secondly, we intend to utilize the underlying stochastics, represented by the quality of life experiments $X_{jt+1}(\cdot)$, in the following way. As it has been mentioned in the text before, one could make several hypotheses concerning the adaption of the probability distributions over X, induced by $X_{jt}(\cdot)$, as time evolves. Irrespective of the particular transition law for the quality of life distributions one could ask whether there is a kind of learning process over these probabilities such that the subjective probability distributions would converge against the objective probability distributions over wage rates and quality of life. This problem is well known in the literature on temporary equilibria ("rational expectations", see Blume (1979)).

Finally we intend to modify our model such that one can formulate a tatonnement process to the migration equilibrium in discrete time. This modification is based on the observation that there is a time lag between immigration and adaption of wages. And this could create a movement of wages and migration streams over time similar to the famous "Cobweb" example. By appropriate assumptions one could also hope to model some dynamic phenomena as "migration business cycles" etc. within such a framework.

Chapter IV

Some Remarks Concerning Econometric Modelling of Informational Aspects in International Migration

IV.1 Introduction

It is the purpose of the present chapter to demonstrate how the framework of sequential decision making can be used to specify econometric models which are intended to measure some of the informational aspects in international migration by empirical observations.

The typical observations on which econometric modelling is based are migration decisions which are implemented, such that the endogenous variables – or the variables to be explained – are discrete ones. Thus the appropriate econometric approach has to belong to the field of (econometric) **discrete choice analysis**.

In this context empirical migration studies can be based either on **individual data** or on **aggregate data** about migration behaviour. For both types we will exhaustively discuss a respective example in section IV.2 and IV.3. We claim that each of these examples is well–suited to demonstrate essential features of the econometric model building and estimation procedures for the individual and aggregate data case respectively. A special concern of our presentation will be to demonstrate the problems which must be solved if econometric studies of the informational aspects in international migration are intended to be measurement **with** theory.

At the beginning of this chapter we would like to damp too great expectations concerning the econometric work already done: a good deal of conceptional problems in building econometric models which are founded in the micro–economic approach developed in this book is solved, whereas only a small part of the immense practical tasks, like data collecting and solving complex maximization problems for estimation by the Maximum–Likelihood method, has been solved until now. Nevertheless in our opinion it seems to be a good completion of our theoretically oriented monograph, to present some suggestions in terms of how the microeconomic theory of international migration under incomplete information could be connected with empirical work.

IV.2 An Econometric Model of Individual Remigration Decisions of Guest–Workers

In this section we will present an econometric model which is designed to capture the remigration decisions of guest–workers, who lived in a host-country for a couple of years, into their home–country. In the intended application of this model the host–country would be W–Germany and the home–country would stand for Turkey. The purpose of such an econometric model will be to obtain a quantitative appraisal of some determinants of the individual remigration decision of guest–workers. This seems to be important from a practical point of view with regard to the ongoing debate about various problems in connection with official programs which are intended to increase the willingness for remigration.[51]

The sample we observe is a set of guest–workers[52] $i = 1, \ldots, m$ born in country 1 who lived in country 2 for some years. Let n_i denote the (observable) number of years guest–worker i from this sample stayed in 2 before remigrating to country 1. Each number n_i is interpreted as the result of some specific discrete choice. According to usual econometric practice we assume that the numbers n_i cannot be completely explained by an exhaustive list of explanatory variables, and therefore are regarded as realizations of a (positive integer–valued) random variable N_i.

Now let us design a sequential decision model which allows us to specify a functional relation

$$\text{Prob}\,[N_i = n_i] = h(z_i; \nu)(i = 1, \ldots, m) \tag{1}$$

with a vector z_i of (observable) personal characteristics of the i–th guest–worker, and an unobservable parameter vector ν_i. This model has the following structure as illustrated by the "decision" tree below.

[51]For a survey of those debates in W–Germany see Hönekopp, E. (1987).

[52]We utilize here the same indexation convention for the countries as in chapter II.

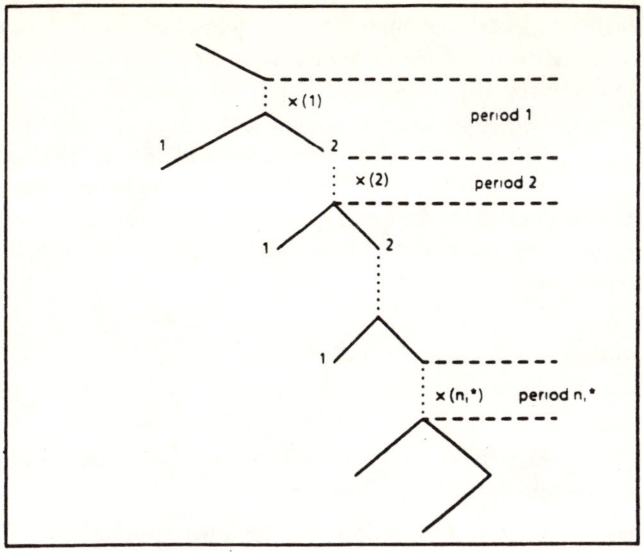

Figure 12: A guest–worker's decision tree

Here $\{x(t)\}_{t=1}^{n_i^*}$ is a real–valued stochastic process of quality–of–life–indices $x(t)$ the guest–worker may experience in his t^{th} year of living in country 2. n_i^* is the maximum number of years i is allowed to live as a guest–worker in country i (e. g. if 65 is his retirement age, we assume that he must leave country 2 at the end of the year when he has reached 65; n_i^* is then supposed to be equal to 65 minus i's age when coming to country 2 as a guest–worker). As it can be seen from the drawing above at the beginning of each of the periods $t = 1, \ldots, n_i^*$ after having observed $x(t)$ the guest–worker has the options "1 $\equiv$ remigrate to country 1 and staying there for the rest of his life" and "2 $\equiv$ stay in country 2 for at least one more period and thus getting the option to decide between '1' and '2' after having observed $x(t+1)$". In period n_i^*+1 his only option is "1", according to institutional restrictions.

Concerning the (subjective) probability law of the process $\{x(t)\}_{t=1}^{n_i^*}$ we assume

(A.1) a) All $x(t)$ are identically normally distributed with mean μ and variance σ^2,

b) $\{x(t)\}$ is a homogeneous Markov process with normal transition probability density; i.e. the conditional density of $x(t)$ given $x(t-1) = x_{t-1}$ is normal with mean $\mu(1-\rho)+\rho x_{t-1}$ and variance $\sigma^2(1-\rho^2)$, where ρ is the correlation coefficient between $x(t)$ and $x(t-1)$.

The normal distribution assumption is introduced for computational convenience. The Markovian assumption then means that $x(t)$ can be predicted partially by the relation $x(t) = \rho x(t-1) + \epsilon(t)$, where $\epsilon(t)$ is (normally) distributed independently of $x(t-1)$. This seems to be a reasonably simplified assumption concerning the guest–workers' (subjective) expectation formation about the quality of life index.

Beside the subjective expectations about the non-pecuniary returns in a country, the second key factor assumed to influence i's remigration behaviour is the per-period real income $y_{1t}^{(i)}$ and $y_{2t}^{(i)}$ in country 1 and country 2 rsp. in country-2-currency. Again – like in the previous chapters – we suppose that income $y_{jt}^{(i)}$ can only be gained by living in country j during period t. To simplify calculations, we will assume that a guest-worker still has infinitely many periods to live after remigration, independently of the period of return. Thus $y_{1t}^{(i)}$ must be considered for $t = 1, \ldots, n_i^*, \ldots$ whereas only finitely many $y_{2t}^{(i)}$, $t = 1, \ldots, n_i^*$ must be taken into account. The crucial assumption concerning the income streams is introduced below:

(A.2) The guest-worker i is completely informed about $y_{1t}^{(i)}$, $t = 1, 2, \ldots, n_i^*, \ldots$ and about $y_{2t}^{(i)}$, $t = 1, 2, \ldots, n_i^*$.

This admittedly very restrictive assumption is introduced as a first approximation. At the end of the section we will discuss how to weaken it.

Then we may define a state $s(t)$ of period t of the guest-worker's decision process as either $s(t) = y_{1t}^{(i)}$, if he is living in country 1 during period t, or as $s(t) = (y_{2t}^{(i)}, x(t))$ if he is living in country 2 during period t. Thus we obtain time-dependent state spaces. More concretely the state space is given by

$$S_t = S_{1t} \cup S_{2t} \tag{2}$$

with

$$S_{1t} = \{y_{1t}\}, \qquad t = 1, \ldots, n_i^*, n_i^* + 1, \ldots$$

$$S_{2t} = \left[\begin{array}{ll} \{y_{2t}^{(i)}\} \times \mathbf{R}, & t = 1, \ldots, n_i^* \\ \{(0,0)\}, & t \geq n_i^* + 1. \end{array} \right.$$

The per-period-utility function $u_t : S_t \to \mathbf{R}$ is supposed to be of the following simple form

(A.3)

$$u_t(s) = \left[\begin{array}{lll} y_{1t}^{(i)} & \text{if} \quad s = y_{1t}^{(i)} \in S_{1t} & \\ y_{2t}^{(i)} + \alpha x_t, & \text{if} \quad s = (y_{2t}^{(i)}, x_t) \in S_{2t} & \text{with} \quad \alpha > 0. \end{array} \right.$$

I. e. we assume that, if individual i is living in his home-country, only his income is utility-relevant whereas if i is living in country 2, his income and the higher (if $x_t > 0$) or lower (if $x_t < 0$) standard of the quality of life compared with that at home[53] determine his utility. Since we are using the Expected Utility framework, the special linear-additive form of $u(\cdot)$ is a crucial assumption, whereas the mentioned normalization can be made without loss of generality, as $u(\cdot)$ is given uniquely only up to positive affine linear transformations.

[53]In contrast to our previous modelling we interprete x here as the quality of life difference between the host-country and the home-country. Consequently we utilize the normalization "$x = 0$" if the quality of life in country 2 is the same as in country 1.

Now let us characterize the optimal remigration behaviour in this sequential decision model by means of the value functions $V_t(s)$. In order to facilitate the formal presentation we use the following abbreviations:

$$\overline{y}_{1t}^{(i)} := \sum_{\tau=t}^{\infty} \beta^{\tau-1} y_{1\tau}^{(i)} \tag{3}$$

where β, with $0 < \beta < 1$, is the discounting factor, and

$$\begin{aligned} B_t(x) \; := \; & \alpha x + \beta(2\pi\sigma^2)) - 1/2 \cdot \\ & \int V_{t+1}(y_{2t+1}^{(i)}, x') \exp\left[-\frac{x' - \mu(1-\rho) - \rho x}{2\sigma^2(1-\rho^2)}\right] dx'. \end{aligned} \tag{4}$$

Then it can be checked easily that

$$V_{n_i^*+1}(s) = \overline{y}_{1,n_i^*+1} \quad (s \in S_{1,n_i^*+1}) \tag{5}$$

and for $t < (n_i^* + 1)$

$$V_t(s) = \left[\begin{array}{ll} \overline{y}_{it}^{(i)}, & \text{for} \quad s \in S_{1t} \\ \max\{\overline{y}_{1t}^{(i)}, y_{2t}^{(i)} + B_t(x)\}, & \text{for} \quad s = (y_{2t}^{(i)}, x) \in S_{2t}) \end{array} \right. \tag{6}$$

As a main result we obtain the following characterization of the optimal remigration behavior

Proposition IV.2.1: *There is a sequence* $\left\{\hat{x}^{(i)}\right\}_{t=1}^{n_i^*}$ *of "reservation"-life-quality indices, such that guest-worker i will remigrate in period t from 2 to 1 for* $x_t^{(i)}$ *iff*

$$x_t^{(i)} \leq \hat{x}_t^{(i)} \tag{7}$$

Here the $\hat{x}_t^{(i)}$ *are uniquely determined by the equations*

$$B_t(\hat{x}_t^{(i)}) = \overline{y}_{1t}^{(i)} - y_{2t}^{(i)}. \tag{8}$$

The proof is given in the appendix A.IV.2.

Now we will change from purely theoretical reasoning about i's remigration behaviour to actual, observed remigration behaviour of a guest-worker i in country 2 born in country 1 as a result of the optimal remigration strategy described in our sequential decision model: in other words, using our sequential decision model we would be able to predict (not necessarily correctly!) the actual remigration behaviour of i, if we knew

i) the income sequences $y_1^{(i)} := \left\{y_{1t}^{(i)}\right\}_{t=1}^{\infty}$ and $y_2^{(i)} := \left\{y_{2t}^{(i)}\right\}_{t=1}^{n_i^*}$

ii) the parameters α, β, μ and ρ

iii) the actual quality of life indices $x_1^{(i)}, \ldots, x_n^{(i)}$.

Concerning i) we assume that we can calculate reasonable proxies for $y_i^{(i)}$ and $y_2^{(i)}$ by observing a list of personal characteristics z_i (this will be discussed in more detail below). With respect to ii) we treat the parameters as unknown values which we want to estimate from data about actual remigration behavior. Concerning iii) let us regard the quality of life indices $x_t^{(i)}$ as determined by an objective random experiment which 'produces' the life quality for any guest–worker from country 1 in country 2 in any period of the considered history of the economy (compare this thought experiment with a similar construction in the model of chap. III.). More precisely with respect to iii) we assume

(A.4) There is a sequence $\{X(k)\}_{k=1}^{\infty}$ of stochastically independent identically distributed random variables $X(k)$, with c.d.f. $G(\cdot;\gamma)$ such that the actual quality of life indices $x_1^{(i)}, \ldots, x_{1n_i^*}^{(i)}$ the guest–worker i may experience in country 2 are realizations of a subsequence $\left\{X(k_t^{(i)})\right\}_{t=1}^{n_i^*}$. The c.d.f. $G(\cdot;\gamma)$ is supposed to be known to the econometrician up to a parameter vector γ.

It should be emphasized furthermore that we do not presuppose any connection between the objective stochastic law of the process $\{X(k)\}$ and the subjective probabilistic judgement about $\{x(t)\}$ as assessed by the individual guest–worker (and formulated in assumption (A.1)).

Now we are ready to derive the following obvious result concerning the specification of the remigration probability given in (1):

Proposition IV.2.2: *Suppose assumptions (A.1),..., (A.4) are fulfilled. Then the probability that guest worker i will remain exactly n_i periods in country 2 before remigration is specified by the following relation*

$$\begin{aligned} Prob\,[N_i = n_i] &= h(z_i, \nu) \\ &= G(\hat{x}_{n_i+1}^{(i)});\gamma) \cdot \prod_{t=1}^{n_i} \left(1 - G\left(\hat{x}_t^{(i)};\gamma\right)\right) \end{aligned} \tag{9}$$

where $\nu := (\alpha, \beta, \mu, \sigma, \rho, \gamma)$.

The dependence on z_i and $(\alpha, \beta, \mu, \sigma, \rho, \gamma)$ is given via the reservation qualities $\hat{x}_t^{(i)}$ determined by equation (8), and the vector z_i denotes data about i allowing the construction of proxies for the income sequences $y_1^{(i)}$ and $y_2^{(i)}$.

This result yields the base for econometric estimation. To make this more precise we need an additional assumption concerning properties of the sample of the m guest–workers in question.

(A.5) a) The guest–workers $i = 1, \ldots, m$ we observe can be regarded as a random sample concerning their individual actual sequences of quality of life indices $\left\{\{X(k_t^{(i)})\}_{t=1}^{n_i^*};\ i = 1, \ldots, m\right\}$.

b) The sample is homogeneous with respect to the parameters $\alpha, \beta, \mu, \sigma$ and ρ.

Whereas (A.5)a) is a requirement for the sampling procedure, assumption (A.5)b) is a hypothesis which serves as a first approximation but should be tested empirically. A priori, of course, we would expect that each of these parameters vary within the population. A possible way to manage the difficulties associated with heterogeneity will be discussed below. But let us first use (A.5) to complete the description of the econometric model.

Proposition IV.2.3: *Suppose assumptions (A.1),..., (A.5) are fulfilled. Then, given the realizations $n_1, \ldots, n_m$ of the years the guest–workers $i = 1, \ldots, m$ have stayed in country 2 before remigration to country 1, the likelihood of the parameter vector $\nu = (\alpha, \beta, \mu, \sigma, \rho, \gamma)$ is given by*

$$L(\nu; n_1, \ldots, n_m) = \prod_{i=1}^{m} h(z_i, \nu) \tag{10}$$

with $h(z_i; \nu)$ as specified in (9).

Now let us come back to the problem of heterogeneity (which is excluded by assumption (A.5)b)[54]: Instead of assuming that e. g. the weight factor α is constant in the population we may suppose that it is the realization of a random variable $\tilde{\alpha}$ distributed according to some c.d.f. $\Phi_{\tilde{\alpha}}(\cdot; \bar{\alpha})$ with some unknown parameter α, and similarly for all or some of the remaining parameters in ν.

Then $h(z_i; \nu)$ would be the conditional probability that guest–worker i stays n_i years before remigration, given $\tilde{\nu} = \nu$. The expression $\overline{h}(z_i; \overline{\nu}) := \int h(z_i; \nu) d\Phi_{\tilde{\nu}}(\nu; \overline{\nu})$ would then be the unconditional probability for the event $\{N_i = n_i\}$, and instead of the likelihood (10) we would get the formula

$$L(\overline{\nu}; n_1, \ldots, n_m) = \prod_{i=1}^{m} \overline{h}(z_i, \overline{\nu}) \tag{10'}$$

Even though this is, from a theoretical point of view, a satisfactory way to relax the restrictive homogeneity assumption (A.5)b) we will not pursue this way here because of the obviously immense additional practical (=numerical) problems of this approach.

After having established the econometric model for the remigration decision we will now systematically discuss some more practical problems that are closely connected with the application of this model.

1. As can be seen from (A.3) we cannot expect to identify α and σ uniquely by observing remigration behaviour based on a utility function which is determined only up to positive affine–linear transformations. Thus we must introduce an identifying assumption, and it seems to suggest itself to set $\sigma = 1$.

2. Since the parameters will be estimated by the Maximum–Likelihood method, we still have to specify the functional form of the c.d.f. $G(\cdot; \gamma)$. According to the standard procedure of discrete–choice–analysis we propose here the logistic c.d.f. with location parameter a and scale parameter b,

$$G(x; a, b) = \{1 + \exp[-(x-a)/b]\}^{-1} = 1 - \{1 + \exp[(x-a)/b]\}^{-1} \tag{11}$$

[54]Compare in this context a similar procedure to deal with this problem in Gotz/McCall (1984).

The shape of this distribution is similar to the shape of the normal distribution but it is easier to handle than the normal c.d.f. since for the calculation of G no numerical integration must be implemented. The variance of G is equal to $b^2\pi^2/3$. It seems worthwhile to remark that with this assumption concerning the objective distribution of the quality of life the essential difference to the assumed subjective probabilistic judgement of the quality–of–life indices is that we allow some stochastic dependence on the subjective level, whereas objectively we postulate stochastic independence.

3. The main computational problem which must be solved if the parameters will be estimated by maximum likelihood is the fact that there does not exist an explicit functional expression for the likelihood function. The reason is the intricate dependence of the critical values $\hat{x}_t^{(i)}$ on the parameters α, β, μ and ρ. The values $\hat{x}_t^{(i)}$ are only determined by an iterative procedure according to equation (8). More precisely: for each $(\alpha, \beta, \mu, \rho)$ the value functions $V_t(\cdot)$ can be determined from (3) and (4). With the help of $V_t(\cdot)$ the $\hat{x}_t^{(i)}(\alpha, \beta, \mu, \rho)$ may be computed by solving for each t equation (8). This makes it clear that we can solve the maximization problem for the likelihood function only by a complex numerical procedure.[55]

4. Our final remarks concern the data problem. More concretely, how can the sequences $y_1^{(i)} = \left\{y_{1t}^{(i)}\right\}_{t=1}^{\infty}$ and $y_2^{(i)} = \{y_{2t}^{\infty}\}_{t=1}^{\infty}$ of incomes $y_{1t}^{(i)}$ and $y_{2t}^{(i)}$ that guest–worker i uses as the basis of his pecuniary calculations for his remigration decision be estimated? Obviously the most satisfactory method would be to ask i for his personal income estimation. But since at the moment no such questionnaires exist to the best of our knowledge, some method has to be invented on how we can construct proxies for these incomes. At the moment we only have a preliminary idea which will be sketched immediately.

   There exist some official statistics about Turkish remigrants from West–Germany[56] from which individual data about n_i and z_i = (age at the date of remigration; sex; family status; education; qualifications; job history; planning for the time after remigration; income situation; savings; etc.) may be obtained. Combining these datas with information about typical careers of Turkish guest–workers and remigrants it seems to be possible to construct the needed income–data. It should be noted that not the incomes actually to be earned must be estimated but the income–estimations which the guest–workers are supposed to use. Insofar it is only crucial to fit the trends of those estimations roughly, and to prove the robustness of the parameter estimation against variations of the underlying data.

[55] At the moment there exist first experiences with such a procedure for the case where we have set $\mu = 0$, $\rho = 0$, $b = 1$, and with fixed discounting factors β, such that only α and a have to be estimated. These experiences encourage us to pursue this approach further; concrete results will be published elsewhere.

[56] The "Institut für Arbeitsmarkt- und Berufsforschung" (Nürnberg) made an inquiry among such remigrants in 1984 from which a set of individual data may be obtained; compare Hönekopp (1987).

IV.3 A Decision Theoretically Founded Econometric Model of Aggregate Guest–Worker Migration

IV.3.1 Introductory Remarks

Here we want to present an econometric model which is designed to explain aggregate migration and remigration flows from and to countries sending guest–workers to W–Germany. An essential part of the structural parameters of the model rely on a sequential decision model, more concretely on a MAB model of international migration, as it has been treated in chap. I.3. Therefore concrete numerical estimations of these parameters must be discussed in the light of this theory. The data which should be used are (aggregate) numbers of migrants and remigrants from the main sending countries of guest–workers to Germany: Italy, Greece, Turkey, Spain and Portugal,[57] from 1963 to 1984. As aggregate data over a rather long time period are intended to be used, it seems necessary to take account of the effects of migratory movements on the German and the sending countries' labour markets (in this context compare our introductory remarks in chap. III).

We will use here a very crude labour market theory: we will derive wage functions from Cobb–Douglas production functions using the marginal productivity theory of labour. It should be stressed furthermore that our model is only a partial equilibrium model, since we have not yet been able to model the whole European labour market because of the still insufficient data situation, or at least to model the market for guest–workers between all sending and receiving European countries. For example our model is not concerned with the effects of guest–worker migration from Spain to France, nor from Italy to Switzerland etc. or the guest–worker remigration from those (and other) sending countries to W–Germany. This restriction has to be given attention when interpreting the estimation results. For an estimation bias resulting from not taking account of the interdependencies between all labour markets cannot be excluded a priori.

IV.3.2 An Econometric Model for Aggregate Guest–Worker Migration

As we wish to demonstrate clearly the (micro–)economic foundation, the additional statistical aspects of this model and the preliminary empirical findings, it seems appropriate to present the model in three subsections:

a) The Economic Model

We consider a host–country, indexed by o, to which in each period t guest–workers from various sending countries $1, \ldots, j, \ldots n$ migrate (temporarily or for good), and from which a portion of these guest–workers remigrates in each period to their home countries.

[57]Because of missing exact information Yugoslavian guest–worker migration cannot be analysed here.

For the migration flows from j to o and back from o to j and for the stocks of 'actives' in j or of guest–workers from j in o the following identities hold:

$$l_{jt} = l_{j,t-1} - m_{jt} + r_{jt} + g_{jt} \tag{12}$$
$$l_{ojt} = l_{oj,t-1} + m_{jt} - r_{jt} + g_{ojt} \tag{13}$$

Here we make use of the following symbols:

l_{jt} := number of 'active' individuals[58] in j at the end of period t

m_{jt} := number of active migrants from j to o during period t

r_{jt} := number of active remigrants from o to j during period t

l_{ojt} := number of active individuals ("guest–workers") from j in o at the end of period t.

g_{jt} and g_{ojt} are the respective residuals. Thus g_{jt} contains the difference between the number of people becoming active persons and the number of those becoming inactive persons, e.g. by death or retirement, and furthermore the difference between the number of remigrants to j from other countries than o. The residual g_{ojt} contains above all the difference between the number of people with nationality of country j, but living in o already for some period, and becoming active persons in period t and the number of people with nationality of country j becoming inactive persons.

In the intended econometric estimation the sending countries j will be Greece, Italy, Turkey, Spain, and Portugal, and the guest–country o will be the FRG.

Beside these counting variables the real wages w_{jt} and w_{ojt} paid on average to workers in country j and to guest–workers from j in country o during period t are still considered.

The core of the model will be to interprete the observable vectors[59]

$$y_t = \left[l_{jt}, l_{ojt}, m_{jt}, r_{jt}, w^*_{jt}, w^*_{ojt}\right]^n_{j=1} \quad \text{for} \quad t = 1, \ldots, T \tag{14}$$

as the realization of a vector–valued Markov process $(Y_t)^n_{t=1}$ with

$$Y_t = \left[L_{jt}, L_{ojt}, M_{jt}, R_{jt}, W^*_{jt}, W^*_{ojt}\right]^n_{j=1} \tag{15}$$

The "link" between the realizations of Y_{t-1} and Y_t that will yield the transition probabilities for the Markov process is a postulated equilibrium mechanism, analogous to that in a cobweb type model. Thus wages w_{jt} and w_{ojt} are assumed to have the property that all active individuals in j and o at the end of period $t-1$ are fully employed. On the other hand w_{jt} and w_{ojt} cause migration and remigration streams between country j and o, and these determine partly new stocks of active individuals in both countries. The dynamic structure of the model may be illustrated graphically as follows:

$$y_{t-1} \rightarrow (l_{j,t-1}, l_{oj,t-1}) \overset{(I)}{\rightarrow} (w_{jt}, w_{ojt}) \overset{(II)}{\rightarrow} (m_{jt}, r_{jt}) \rightarrow y_t \tag{16}$$

[58]In the glossary of the "Statistisches Bundesamt" (Wiesbaden, FRG) these are referred to as 'Erwerbspersonen'.

[59]Here and in the sequel we use the notation: $w^*_{jt} := \ln w_{jt}$ and $w^*_{ojt} := \ln w_{ojt}$.

In the rest of this section we will firstly specify relation (I), and then we will apply the MAB-model of international migration from chap. I.3 and some obvious additional restrictions to obtain a decision theoretically founded specification of (II).

For specifying the link (I) in the above chain, wage functions in countries j and o will be specified by making use of the marginal productivity theory of labour, applied to Cobb-Douglas production functions. We begin by doing this for country o. We assume a production function

$$\text{Output} = \epsilon_o l_{o1}^{\epsilon_1} \ldots l_{on}^{\epsilon_n} L^{\epsilon_{n+1}} K^{\epsilon_{n+2}}$$

where K and L denote the stock of capital and of domestic labour in country o, and where $0 < \epsilon_1, \ldots, \epsilon_{n+2} < 1$ are the respective factor elasticities, and $\epsilon_o > 0$ is a scale parameter. Then the following equation can be derived for the wage w_{ojt}, paid to the guest-workers from j in o in period t

$$\begin{aligned} \ln w_{ojt} &= (\epsilon_j - 1)\lambda_{oj,t-1} + \ln \epsilon_j + \ln \epsilon_o + \epsilon_{n+1} \ln L_{t-1} \\ &\quad + \epsilon_{n+2} \ln K_{t-1} + \sum_{k \neq j} \epsilon_k \lambda_{ok,t-1}. \end{aligned}$$

Here the abbreviations

$$\lambda_{okt} := \ln l_{okt} \quad (k = 1, \ldots, j, \ldots, n), \lambda_{on+1,t} = \ln L_t \tag{17}$$

are used.

If K_t is assumed to be constant $= K$ during the considered time periods $t = 1, \ldots, T$, the wage function for w_{ojt} can be written in a compact form as follows:

$$w_{ojt}^* = \ln w_{ojt} = \alpha_{oj} + \beta_{oj}\lambda_{oj,t-1} + \sum_{\substack{k=1 \\ k \neq j}}^{n+1} \epsilon_k \lambda_{ok,t-1} + e_{ojt} \tag{18}$$

with the meaning of the symbols

$$\begin{aligned} \alpha_{oj} &:= \ln \epsilon_j + \ln \epsilon_o + \epsilon_{n+2} \ln K, \\ \beta_{oj} &:= \epsilon_j - 1, \\ e_{ojt} &\equiv \text{residual term.} \end{aligned}$$

In a similar but more simple way the function determining the wage w_{jt} paid to the workers in j during period t can be derived as

$$w_{jt}^* = \ln w_{jt} = \alpha_j + \beta_j \lambda_{j,t-1} + e_{jt}, \tag{19}$$

where $\lambda_{j,t-1} = \ln l_{j,t-1}$, and $(1 + \beta_j)$ is the factor elasticity of labour in country j, α_j is a linear combination of the logarithm of this elasticity, the capital stock in j (assumed to be constant too) and of the scale parameter of the production function, and e_{jt} is a residual term. As usual the residuals e_{ojt} and e_{jt} are supposed to capture the "random" influence on the wages; they will be specified more concretely in 3.2.

Next let us consider a fixed sending country j. We intend to derive now the stochastic dependence of the migration and remigration flows from j to o and back from o to j on the wages w_{jt} and w_{ojt} for a specific time period t; compare (II) in the diagram (16). For this sake we proceed in three steps: first, (i), the Multi–Armed–Bandit model of the individual migration/remigration decisions from chap. I.3 will be applied to derive conditions for individual migration and remigration; secondly, (ii), individual migration and remigration probabilities will be calculated from these conditions, and thirdly, (iii), by assuming the migration/re–(re)migration flows to obey a binomial distribution law specific dependencies of the probability distributions for the random variables M_{jt} and R_{jt} on the wages w_{ojt} and w_{jt} will be obtained.

(i) We consider a fixed time period t, and define the sets

$$
\begin{aligned}
I_{jt} &:= \text{the set of all workers in } j \text{ at the beginning of period } t,\\
I_{ojt} &:= \text{the set of all guest–workers from } j \text{ in } o \text{ at the beginning of period } t.
\end{aligned}
$$

At first let us specify the migration behaviour of a worker $i \in I_{jt}$. For this sake we adopt the sequential decision framework, more precisely, the special MAB framework that has been developed in chap. I.3.2.[60] with one modification and two specialisations. The modification concerns the reward function; instead of the wage income to enter into the reward linearly here a logarithmic form is supposed. I.e. instead of the specification in chapt. I.3.2. (compare figure 1, and formula (27) in I.3.2) we postulate here

$$
\begin{aligned}
u_r(s_{or}) &:= -c_r, \\
u_r(w_r) &:= \ln w_r - k_r = w_r^* - k_r, \\
u_r(w_r, x_r) &:= \ln w_r + x_r = w_r^* + x_r \quad (r = j, o).
\end{aligned}
\tag{20}
$$

Some calculations with alternative functional forms have shown that the logarithmic form is best suited to our purposes.

The specializations are concerned here with the concrete form of the probability distribution $G_r(\cdot)$, $r = j, o$ for the quality of life index x_r, expressing the migrants' incomplete information. For $r = j$ we assume $G_j(\cdot)$ to be concentrated at $x_j = 0$, whereas for $r = o$ we postulate the existence of a strictly positive real number $\overline{x}_{oj}$ such that $G_o(\cdot)$ is concentrated at $-\overline{x}_{oj}$ and $\overline{x}_{oj}$ with jumps of $1/2$ at $-\overline{x}_{oj}$ and $\overline{x}_{oj}$. I.e. it is assumed that the migrant $i \in I_{jt}$ considers x_o as a net index of the higher or lower standard of the quality of life in country o compared with that in his home country j, and that he expects only $-\overline{x}_{oj}$ or $\overline{x}_{oj}$ as possible realizations of x_o, each with probability $1/2$. – Finally we assume $k_j = 0$, i.e. staying at home causes no migration costs.

Then we may obtain by using the results in Prop. I.3.2:

Proposition IV.3.1: *If the worker $i \in I_{jt}$ is supposed to be completely informed about the wages w_{jt} and w_{ojt}, and if the relation*

$$
w_{ojt}^* - \overline{x}_{oj} < w_{jt}^* \tag{21}
$$

[60]The reader is urgently invited to reread that section, since the microeconomic foundation of the econometric model bases heavily on this, and we will be rather short on this point here.

holds, then i will migrate from j to o during period t, iff

$$k_{ojt} < \gamma \left[w^*_{ojt} - w^*_{jt}\right] + (1-\gamma)\overline{x}_{oj} \qquad (22)^{61}$$

with $\gamma := (1-\beta/2)/(1-\beta)$

Proof: See Appendix A.IV.3.

Next let us specify the migration behaviour of a guest-worker $i \in I_{ojt}$. Again we adopt the special MAB framework of chapt. I.3.2. modified and specialized as outlined above. This yields:

Proposition IV.3.2: *If the guest-worker* $i \in I_{ojt}$ *is completely informed about the wages* w_{jt} *and* w_{ojt}*, and about the quality of life index* x_{ojt}*, then i will remigrate from o to j during period t iff*

$$x_{ojt} < w^*_{jt} - w^*_{ojt} \qquad (23)$$

Proof: See Appendix A.IV.3.

(ii) After having derived in (i) conditions which characterize the individual migration and remigration behaviour in a supposed MAB framework, we will now turn to the empirical analysis of this model. Whereas it was supposed that each worker $i \in I_{jt}$ is completely informed about wages w_{ojt} and w_{jt} and his costs k_{ojt} of migrating from j to o during period t, and that each guest-worker $i \in I_{ojt}$ is completely informed about w_{ojt} and w_{jt}, and additionally about the quality of life index x_{ojt}, the empirical analyst of this model will typically not be so well informed. Naturally his "incomplete information" will be about the indices of the migration costs and about the quality of life index, more specifically about: k_{ojt} and x_{ojt}, and furthermore about the subjective estimate $\overline{x}_{oj}$ and about the discount factor β (rsp. to γ; compare Proposition IV.3.1).

A possible way out of this informational deficit which will be pursued in this chapter consists of the following steps:

(A): It is assumed that all workers $i \in I_{jt}$ are homogeneous with respect to the subjective factors of the MAB problem x_{oj} and β (and that of course they all have the same utility function (20)). Then $\overline{x}_{oj}$ and β rsp. γ are treated as unknown parameters of the econometric model.

(B): a) The workers $i \in I_{jt}$ may be different with respect to their migration costs k_{ojt}, in the following sense: there is a random variable K_{ojt} with c.d.f. F_{ojt} such that each k_{ojt}, $i \in I_{jt}$, is a realization of K_{ojt}; and similarly:

b) The (guest)workers $i \in I_{ojt}$ may be different with respect to their quality of life indices x_{ojt} in the following sense: there is a random variable X_{ojt} with c.d.f. H_{ojt} such that each x_{ojt}, $i \in I_{ojt}$, is a realization of X_{ojt}.

c) The c.d.f.'s F_{ojt} rsp. H_{ojt} will not change during the time periods of observation. That is, we set $F_{ojt} \equiv F_{oj}$ and $H_{ojt} \equiv H_{oj}$ for all t.

---

[61] By k_{ojt} we denote the costs of migration from j to o for $i \in I_{jt}$; this corresponds to k_o in specification (20).

Assumptions (A) and (B) seem to be convenient econometric practice and need no further comment here. Accepting them allows the straightforward derivation of the following propositions concerning the migration and remigration probabilities:

Proposition IV.3.3: *Given the wages w_{jt} and w_{ojt}, then the probability that any $i \in I_{jt}$ will migrate from t to o in period t is equal to*

$$\Pi_j(w^*_{jt}, w^*_{ojt}; \gamma, \overline{x}_{oj}) := F_{oj}[\gamma(w^*_{ojt} - w^*_{jt}) + (1-\gamma)\overline{x}_{oj}]. \tag{24}$$

The result follows easily from (A) and (B) combined with Proposition IV.3.1.

Proposition IV.3.4: *Given the wages w_{jt} and w_{ojt}, then the probability that any $i \in I_{ot}$ will remigrate from o to j in period t is equal to*

$$\Pi_{oj}(w^*_{jt}, w^*_{ojt}) := H_{oj}(w^*_{jt} - w^*_{ojt}). \tag{25}$$

Again this is obvious, by (A), (B) and Proposition IV.3.2.

(iii) We will complete the economic theoretical part of the econometric model by specifying in complete detail the conditional probabilities

$$\text{Prob } [M_{jt} = m_{jt} | w^*_{jt}, w^*_{ojt}, l_{j,t-1}] \quad \text{and} \tag{26}$$

$$\text{Prob } [R_{jt} = r_{jt} | w^*_{jt}, w^*_{ojt}, l_{oj,t-1}]$$

for the stochastic processes M_{jt} of the number of migrants from j to o during t and R_{jt} of remigrants from o to j during t. This specification will be based on the individual migration and remigration probabilities in (24) and (25), and on the following assumptions:

(C.1) Each individual $i \in I_{jt}$ has equal probability $\Pi_j(w_{jt}, w_{ojt}; \gamma, \overline{x}_{oj})$ of migrating from j to o in period t, and for different individuals the events inducing migration are regarded as stochastically independent.

(C.2) Each individual $i \in I_{ojt}$ has equal probability $\Pi_{oj}(w_{jt}, w^*_{ojt})$ of remigrating from o to j in period t, and for different individuals the events inducing remigration are regarded as stochastically independent.

The idea leading to (C.1) and (C.2) is to consider the sets I_{jt} and I_{ojt} of workers in j at the beginning of period t and of guest–workers from j in o at the beginning of t as a sample out of the population of all workers in j at all periods and of all guest–workers from j at o at all periods and then to look for the individuals with characteristic "migrant from j to o" and "remigrant from o to j". Then it is supposed in (C.1) and in (C.2) that these samples are $l_{j,t-1} = |I_{jt}|$ and $l_{oj,t-1} = |I_{ot}|$ independent Bernoulli trials with success probability $\Pi_j(w^*_{jt}, w^*_{ojt}; \gamma, \overline{x}_{oj})$ and $\Pi_{oj}(w^*_{jt}, w^*_{ojt})$.

Since $l_{j,t-1} = |I_{jt}|$ rsp. $l_{oj,t-1} = |I_{ojt}|$ we get from (C.1) rsp. (C.2) the following characterizations of the conditional probabilities of M_{jt} and R_{jt}.

Proposition IV.3.5: *a) The conditional probability that the (discrete) random variable* M_{jt} *takes the value* m_{jt}*, given* w^*_{jt}*,* w^*_{ojt} *and* $l_{j,t-1}$ *is given by*

$$\begin{aligned}\text{Prob}\,[M_{jt} = m_{jt} | w^*_{jt}, w^*_{ojt}, l_{j,t-1}] &= \qquad (27)\\ &= \begin{bmatrix} l_{j,t-1} \\ m_{jt} \end{bmatrix} \left[F_{oj}(\gamma(w^*_{ojt} - w^*_{jt}) + (1-\gamma)\overline{x}_{oj})\right]^{m_{jt}} \\ &\cdot \left[1 - F_{oj}(\gamma(w^*_{ojt} - w^*_{jt}) + (1-\gamma)\overline{x}_{oj})\right]^{l_{j,t-1} - m_{jt}}\end{aligned}$$

b) The conditional probability that the random variable R_{jt} *takes the value* r_{jt}*, given* w^*_{jt}*,* w^*_{ojt} *and* $l_{oj,t-1}$ *is given by*

$$\begin{aligned}\text{Prob}\,[R_{jt} = r_{jt} | w^*_{jt}, w^*_{ojt}, l_{oj,t-1}] &= \\ &= \begin{bmatrix} l_{oj,t-1} \\ r_{jt} \end{bmatrix} \left[H_{oj}(w^*_{jt} - w^*_{ojt})\right]^{r_{jt}} \qquad (28) \\ &\cdot \left[1 - H_{oj}(w^*_{jt} - w^*_{ojt})\right]^{l_{j,t-1} - r_{jt}}\end{aligned}$$

Finally let us summarize the results of this subsection in which we have tried to specify the decision theoretical foundation of an econometric model of migration/remigration flows.

The endogenous variables of the model are comprised in the vector

$$y_t = (l_{jt}, l_{ojt}, m_{jt}, r_{jt}, w^*_{jt}, w^*_{ojt}).$$

The predetermined variables are

$$l_{j,t-1}, l_{oj,t-1}, \quad \text{and} \quad l_{ok,t-1} \quad (k = 1, \ldots, n+1,\ k \neq j)$$

with $l_{on+1,t} = L_t$.

The meaning of the variables is given in the rows following (12) and (13), and preceding (14). Our model has a dynamic structure, more precisely a recursive one (compare the chain-relation (16)). And it consists of six equations: (12), (13), (18), (19) and (27), (28).

(12) and (13) are the counting equations "explaining" l_{jt} and l_{ojt}. Using the marginal productivity theory of labour applied to Cobb–Douglas production functions yields the wage equations (18) and (19) for w^*_{jt} and w^*_{ojt}. The most important part of the model – from the perspective of this volume's subject – are the equations (27) and (28) determining m_{jt} and r_{jt}; and these equations (27) and (28) are derived by three main steps: i) from an individual decision–theoretical approach in the special MAB framework, which has been developed in chap. I.3., ii) from separating the unobservable variables determining the implied migration/remigration behaviour into unknown parameters of the model (which are assumed to be homogeneous for all migrants/remigrants) and into random variables (from the empirical analyst's point of view) with some postulated stochastic law; this yields our individual migration and remigration probabilities. And iii) from postulating

each observed migration and remigration respectively to be the realization of a Bernoulli process with success probabilities according to those derived under ii).

b) Statistical Aspects of the Model and the Likelihood Function

In this section the stochastic part of the model, namely:

(i) the residuals g_{jt} and g_{ojt} in equations (12) and (13),

(ii) the residuals e_{jt} and e_{ojt} in equations (18) and (19), and

(iii) the c.d.f. F_{oj} and H_{oj} in equations (27) and (28),

must be further specified, in order to obtain a form of the model which can be estimated by econometric methods.

(i) Since equations (12) and (13) will play only the role of completing the model, it suffices here to suppose

(D.1) There is a $2T$–dimensional (discrete) random vector with probability function Φ_{oj} such that $(g_{j1}, \dots, g_{jT}, g_{oj1}, \dots, g_{ojT})$ is a realization of that random vector.

Notice that we do not need any specific distributional assumption, neither independence nor anything else.[62]

(ii) Since it is intended to estimate the wage functions, more specific assumptions are needed with regard to the residuals e_{ojt} and e_{jt}. Following usual econometric practice we suppose without any further comment:

(D.2) The residuals e_{jt} and e_{ojt} are pairwise and serially uncorrelated and identically normally distributed with zero mean and variances σ_j^2 rsp. σ_{oj}^2.

(iii) According to assumption (B) in part a) of this section, the c.d.f. F_{oj} and H_{oj} describe the empirical analyst's opinion on how the costs of migrations k_{ojt} from country j to country o are distributed in the population of country j, and on how the actual quality of life indices x_{ojt} are distributed in the population of guest–workers from j in country o. As a reasonable compromise between prior plausibility and computational manageability we make the following assumptions.

(D.3) a) The random variable K_{oj} (with realizations k_{ojt}) has a Weibull–distribution with scale parameter 1 and shape parameter c, $c > 0$, i.e.

$$F_{oj}(k; c) = 1 - \exp[(-k)^c], \quad \text{for} \quad k \geq 0. \tag{29}$$

b) The random variable X_{oj} (with realizations x_{ojt}) is logistically distributed with location parameter a and scale parameter b, i.e.

$$\begin{aligned} H_{oj}(x; a, b) &= 1 - \{1 + \exp[(x - a)/b]\}^{-1} \\ &= \{1 + \exp[-(x - a)/b]\}^{-1} \end{aligned} \tag{30}$$

[62] We would have to make more specific assumptions if we wanted to make predictions or simulations with our model; but (D.1) is sufficient for estimation.

The density function $F_{oj'}(\cdot; c)$ of the Weibull–distribution (29) has (for alternative values of c) a shape that is sketched in the following figure below.

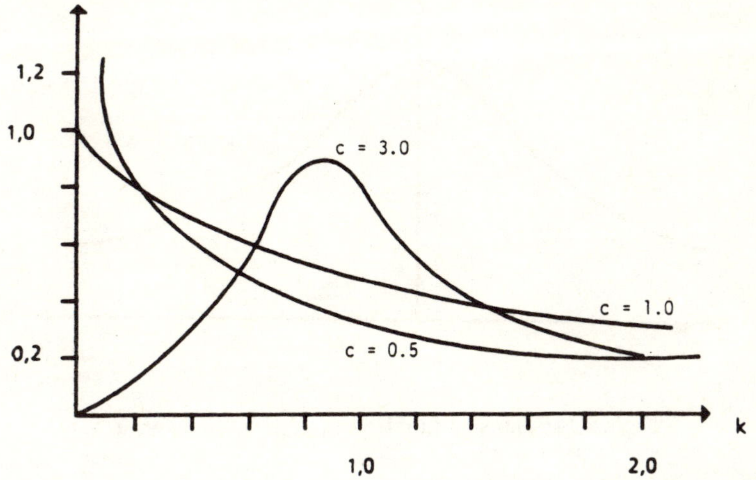

Figure 13: Density function of $F_{oj}(\cdot)$ for selected parameter values

It seems reasonable to expect a shape parameter c near 3.0, i.e. unimodal with mode essentially greater than zero. The mode of $F_{oj}(\cdot; c)$ is given by $(1 - 1/c)(1/c)$ for $c \geq 1$ and by 0 for $c \leq 1$ (see e.g. Hastings/Peacock (1975), p. 126).

Thus (D.3)a) implies that the costs of migrating from j to o are non–negative for all members of the population in country j, and that the greatest fraction of the population has costs around the mode of the distribution, whereas smaller and greater migration costs are relatively rare in the population.

Assuming that the random variable X_{oj} whose realizations are the life–quality indices x_{ojt} which the individuals $i \in I_{ojt}$ experience as guest–workers in o is logistically distributed with location paramter a and scale parameter b amounts to suppose the following approximately normal shape of the density $H'_{oj}(\cdot; a, b)$ of X_{oj}:

Whereas the curtosis of a normal variate is equal to 3.0, that of a logistic variate is 4.2, i.e. for identical variances the fourth moment about the mean of the logistic variate is 1.4 times greater than that of the normal variate.

We have preferred to choose the logistic shape for the c.d.f. of X_{oj} for computational convenience. On the other hand we believe that the assumption of a c.d.f. with a shape like the normal or the logistic variate is an a priori appropriate hypothesis about the distribution of the quality of life indices the guest–workers $i \in I_{ojt}$ actually experience. – For the interpretation of the results of the estimation we mention, that $E(X_{oj}) = a$ and $\text{var}(X_{oj}) = b^2\pi^2/3$.

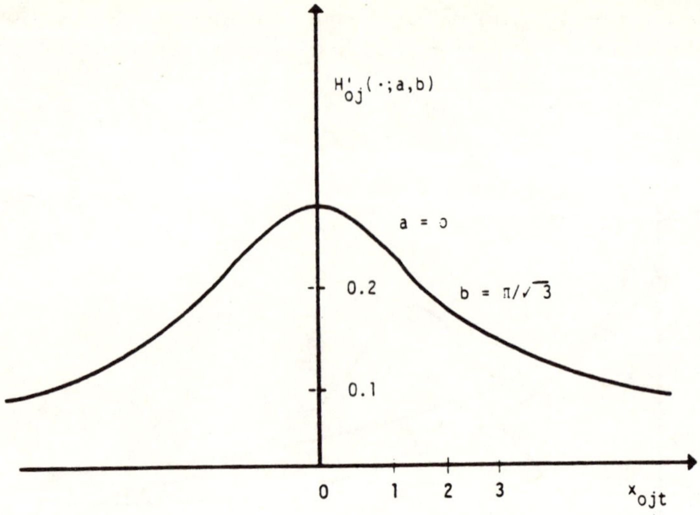

Figure 14: Density function of $H_{oj}(\cdot)$ for given a, b

Now the specification of the econometric model is complete, and we can derive the likelihood function. More precisely, we collect the unknown parameters in the vector[63]

$$\nu = (\overbrace{\alpha_{oj}, \beta_{oj}, \epsilon_j, \ldots, \epsilon_{j-1}, \epsilon_{j+1}, \ldots, \epsilon_{n+1}, \sigma_{cj}}^{(18)}, \underbrace{\alpha_j, \beta_j, \sigma_j}_{(19)}, \overbrace{\gamma, \overline{x}_{oj}, c}^{(27)}, \underbrace{a, b}_{(28)}) \tag{31}$$

Then the likelihood function $L(\nu; y)$ for a given vector $y = (y_1, \ldots y_T)$ of the endogenous variables $y_t = (l_{jt}, l_{ojt}, m_{jt}, r_{jt}, w^*_{jt}, w^*_{ojt})$ is given by

$$\begin{aligned} L(\nu; y) &= \text{Prob}_\nu[y_1, \ldots, y_T] \qquad (32)\\ &= \text{Prob}_\nu[(l_{j1}, l_{oj1}), \ldots, (l_{jT}, l_{ojT}) | (m_{j1}, r_{j1}), \ldots, (m_{jT}, r_{jT})] \\ &\quad \cdot \text{Prob}_\nu[m_{j1}, \ldots, m_{jT} | (w^*_{j1}, w^*_{oj1}, l_{j1}), \ldots, (w^*_{j1}, w^*_{oj1}, l_{jT})] \\ &\quad \cdot \text{Prob}_\nu[r_{j1}, \ldots, r_{jT} | (w^*_{j1}, w^*_{oj1}, l_{oj1}), \ldots, (w^*_{jT}, w^*_{ojT}, l_{ojT})] \\ &\quad \cdot \text{Prob}_\nu[w^*_{j1}, \ldots, w^*_{jT} | l_{j1}, \ldots, l_{jT}] \\ &\quad \cdot \text{Prob}_\nu[w^*_{oj1}, \ldots, w^*_{ojT} | l_{oj1}, \ldots, l_{ojT}] \\ &= A \cdot \prod_{t=1}^{T} \begin{bmatrix} l_{j,t-1} \\ m_{jt} \end{bmatrix} (1 - \exp[(-\gamma(w^*_{ojt} - w^*_{jt}) - (1-\gamma)\overline{x}_{oj})^c])^{m_{jt}} \\ &\quad \cdot (\exp[(-\gamma(w^*_{ojt} - w^*_{jt}) - (1-\gamma)\overline{x}_{oj})^c])^{l_{j,t-1} - m_{jt}} \\ &\quad \cdot \prod_{t=1}^{T} \begin{bmatrix} l_{oj,t-1} \\ r_{jt} \end{bmatrix} (1 + \exp[(-\frac{1}{b}(w^*_{jt} - w^*_{ojt} - a)])^{r_{jt}} \end{aligned}$$

[63]The ordering of the components of ν corresponds to the equations.

$$\cdot(1+\exp[(\frac{1}{b}(w^*_{jt}-w^*_{ojt}-a)])^{r_{jt}-l_{oj,t-1}}$$

$$\cdot(2\pi)^{-T/2}\cdot\sigma_j^{-T}\prod_{t=1}^{T}\exp\left[\frac{-(w^*_{jt}-\alpha_j-\beta_j\lambda_{j,t-1})^2)}{2\sigma_j^2}\right]$$

$$\cdot(2\pi)^{-T/2}\cdot\sigma_{oj}^{-T}$$

$$\cdot\prod_{t=1}^{T}\exp\left[-\frac{1}{2\sigma_j^*}(w^*_{ojt}-\alpha_{oj}-\beta_{oj}\lambda_{oj,t-1}-\sum_{\substack{k=1\\k\neq j}}^{n+1}\epsilon_k\lambda_{ok,t-1})^2\right]$$

where the expression A is given by

$$\begin{aligned}A &= \Phi_{oj}((l_{j1}-l_{jo}+m_{j1}-r_{j1},l_{oj1}-l_{oj0}-m_{j1}+r_{j1}),\ldots,\\ &\quad \ldots,(l_{jT}-l_{j,T-1}+m_{jT}-r_{jT},l_{oj1}-l_{oj,T-1}-m_{jT}+r_{jT})),\end{aligned}$$

and therefore is independent of the parameter vector ν. By transforming $L(\nu;y)$ into the log–likelihood–function we may state the following Proposition concerning the estimation of the components with the Maximum–Likelihood–Method.

Proposition IV.3.6: *In the econometric model of guest–worker migration/remigration from j to o and vice versa as given by equations (12), (13), (18), (19) and (27), (28), and as specified by assumptions (A), (B), (C) and (D) the unknown parameter vector ν from (31) can be estimated according to the Maximum–Likelihood–Method by solving the following four maximization problems*

(M.1) For the estimation of α_j, β_j and σ_j

$$\max_{\alpha_j,\beta_j,\sigma_j}\left\{-T\ln\sigma_j-\frac{1}{2\sigma_j^2}\sum_{t=1}^{T}(w^*_{jt}-\alpha_j-\beta_j\lambda_{j,t-1})^2\right\}.$$

(M.2) For the estimation of α_{oj}, β_{oj} ϵ_k $(k=1,\ldots,n+1,k\neq j)$, σ_{oj}

$$\max\left\{-T\ln\sigma_{oj}-\frac{1}{2\sigma_{oj}^2}\sum_{t=1}^{T}(w^*_{ojt}-\alpha_{oj}-\beta_{oj}\lambda_{oj,t-1})^2-\sum_{\substack{k=1\\k\neq j}}^{n+1}\epsilon_k\lambda_{ok,t-1})^2\right\}.$$

(M.3) For the estimation of γ, $\overline{x}_{oj}$ and c

$$\max\left\{\sum_{t=1}^{T}m_{jt}\ln(1-\exp[(\gamma(w^*_{jt}-w^*_{ojt})-(1-\gamma)\overline{x}_{oj})^c])\right.$$

$$\left.+(l_{j,t-1}-m_{jt})\cdot c\cdot[\gamma(w^*_{jt}-w^*_{ojt})-(1-\gamma)\overline{x}_{oj}]\right\}.$$

(M.4) For the estimation of a and b

$$\max\left\{\sum_{t=1}^{T}-r_{jt}(1+\exp[(-\frac{1}{b}(w^*_{jt}-w^*_{ojt}-a)])\right.$$

$$+ (r_{jt} - l_{oj,t-1})(1 + \exp[\frac{1}{b}(w^*_{jt} - w^*_{ojt} - a)])\Big\} .$$

Whereas (M.1) and (M.2) are classical maximization problems the problems (M.3) and (M.4) require the solution of some still unsolved numerical procedures.

With the statement of the previous Proposition the presentation of the theoretical part of our econometric model is completed.

CHESTER COLLEGE LIBRARY

Appendix A.I.3

Proof of Proposition I.3.2:

To simplify notation we will use here the following abbreviations

$$\begin{aligned} Z_j(w_j, x_j) &= Z^2 \quad \text{(we omit the index for the region)} \\ Z_j(w_j) &= Z^1 \\ Z_j(s_0) &= Z_0. \end{aligned}$$

a) According to (21) and (22) in chap. I.3.we have

$$Z^2 = (w+x) + \beta V((w,x); Z^2), \tag{1}$$

$$V(w,x) = \max\{Z^2, (w+x) + \beta V((w,x); Z^2)\}. \tag{2}$$

Inserting (1) into (2) we obtain

$$V((w,x), Z^2) = (w+x)/(1-\beta) \tag{3}$$

what implies

$$Z^2 = (w+x) + \beta/(1-\beta) \cdot (w+x) = (w+x)/(1-\beta).$$

b) From (1), (2) and (3) we obtain

$$\begin{aligned} Z^1 &= (w-k) + \beta \int \max\left\{Z^1, \frac{w+x}{1-\beta}\right\} dG(x) \qquad (4) \\ &= (w-k) + \beta Z^1 G((1-\beta)Z^1 - w) + \int_{[(1-\beta)Z^1 - w]} \frac{w+x}{1-\beta} dG(x) \\ &= (w-k) + \beta Z^1 + \beta \int (\frac{w+x}{1-\beta} - Z^1)^+ dG(x), \end{aligned}$$

what implies the desired result.

c) By taking account of (1), (2) and (3) we obtain

$$\begin{aligned} Z^0 &= -c + \beta \int \max\Big\{Z^0, (w-k) \\ &\qquad + \beta \int \max\left\{Z^0, \frac{w+x}{1-\beta}\right\} dG(x)\Big\} dF(w). \end{aligned}$$

By an analogous reasoning as above this equation can be transformed as follows

$$\begin{aligned} Z^0 &= -\frac{c}{1-\beta} + \frac{\beta}{1-\beta} \int \Big(w-k \\ &\qquad + \beta \int \max\left\{Z^0, \frac{w+x}{1-\beta}\right\} dG(x) - Z^0\Big)^+ dF(w). \end{aligned}$$

As the integrand can be transformed furthermore into

$$\left(w - k + \beta Z^0 + \beta \int \left(\frac{w+x}{1-\beta} - Z^0\right)^+ dG(x) - Z^0\right)^+$$

the result follows immediately. Q.E.D.

Proof of Proposition I.3.4:

As the function

$$g_1(x) := ((w+x)/(1-\beta) - Z)^+$$

is convex in x, and the function

$$g_2(w) := \left(w - k + \beta \int \left(\frac{w+x}{1-\beta} - Z\right)^+ dG(x) - (1-\beta)Z\right)^+$$

is convex in w, it follows from a well-known characterization of a m.p.s. (e.g. Lippman/McCall (1982), Theorem 2) that the graphs of $f_2(\cdot)$ and $f_3(\cdot)$ (Figure 2) are shifted to the right with increasing m.p.s. of $F(\cdot)$ and/or $G(\cdot)$, giving the desired result. Q.E.D.

Proof of Proposition I.3.5.:

Taking equation (29), chap. I.3., into account we obtain

$$k_j = w_j + \beta \int \left(\frac{w_j + x_j}{1-\beta} - Z_j(w_j)\right)^+ dG_j(x_j) - (1-\beta)Z_j(w_j). \tag{5}$$

As the right-hand side of (5) is strictly decreasing in $Z_j(w_j)$ we conclude that (with $Z_j^* = \max_{i \neq j} Z_i(s_i)$)

$$Z_j(w_j) > Z_j^* \quad \text{iff} \quad k_j < w_j + \beta \int \left(\frac{w+x}{1-\beta} - Z_j^*\right)^+ dG_j(x_j) - (1-\beta)Z_j^*.$$

As the right-hand side of the inequality is continuous and strictly increasing in w_j we obtain the desired result. Q.E.D.

Appendix A.I.4

Proof of Proposition I.4.1:

It follows from (39) and (40) that for each $z \in R$ the sequence $(f_n)_{n=1}^{\infty}$ of G–integrable functions $f_n(\cdot, z) : X \to \mathbf{R}$ with $f_n(x, z) := \max\{0, (w + v_n(x))/(1-\beta) - z\}$ fulfills the conditions of the Lebesgue–Monotone–Convergence–Theorem. This yields for each z

$$\lim_{n \to \infty} \int_X f_n(x, z) dG(x) = \int_X \max\left\{0, \frac{w + v^*(x)}{1-\beta} - z\right\} dG(x).$$

Therefore we can conclude immediately (41). Q.E.D.

Proof of Lemma I.4.1:

i) Let $x_v(z)$ be given by $v(x_v(z)) = z(1-\beta) - w$. Then x_v is continuous, even differentiable, and increasing in z as $v(\cdot)$ is increasing and differentiable. Notice that $x_v(z^+(\epsilon)) = \overline{x} + \epsilon$, and let analogously be defined: $z^-(\epsilon)$ by $x_v(z - (\epsilon)) = \overline{x} - \epsilon$.

ii) The integral $I(z)$ in (49) can then be written as

$$I(z) = \int_{x_v(z)}^{\overline{x}+\epsilon} v(x) dG_\epsilon(x) + \left(\frac{w}{1-\beta} - z\right)(1 - G_\epsilon(x_v(z))).$$

This shows:

a) For z, $z^-(\epsilon) \leq z < z^+(\epsilon)$, $I(z)$ is continuous.

b) For $z \leq z^-(\epsilon)$ we get: $I(z) = w/(1-\beta) - z +$ "expression not depending on z", and thus $I(\cdot)$ is continuous in this range too; especially $I(\cdot)$ is continuous at $z^-(\epsilon)$.

c) For $z \geq z^+(\epsilon)$ we get $I(z) = 0$, i.e. $I(\cdot)$ is continuous in this range too.

d) Obviously 0 is the limit of $I(z_n)$ with $z_n < z^+(\epsilon)$ and converging to $z^+(\epsilon)$.

iii) Thus f_ϵ is continuous for all z and constant equal to $(w-k)/(1-\beta)$ for $z \geq z^+(\epsilon)$.

iv) For $z \leq z^-(\epsilon)$ $I(\cdot)$ is obviously decreasing.

v) For z, $z^-(\epsilon) < z < z^+(\epsilon)$, $I(\cdot)$ is differentiable $\frac{dI(z)}{dz} = (1 - G_\epsilon(x_v(z))) < 0$, i.e. $I(\cdot)$ is decreasing in this range too.

Q.E.D.

Proof of Lemma I.4.2:

i) We write for short $Z_\epsilon := Z_v(k,\epsilon)$, $\epsilon \geq 0$.

ii) From (51) it follows $Z_0 < z^+(\epsilon)$ for all $k > 0$; thus $f_\epsilon(Z_0) \gtreqless f(z)$ for all z with $z \gtreqless Z_0$, as long as $k > 0$.

iii) Because of $Z_\epsilon = f_\epsilon(Z_\epsilon)$ we get: $Z_0 = Z_\epsilon \Leftrightarrow f_\epsilon(Z_\epsilon) = Z_0$.

iv) Similarly $Z_0 > Z_\epsilon \Leftrightarrow f_\epsilon(Z_0) < f_\epsilon(Z_\epsilon) < Z_0$ and $Z_0 < Z_\epsilon \Leftrightarrow f_\epsilon(Z_0) > f_\epsilon(Z_\epsilon) > Z_0$.

Q.E.D.

Proof of Lemma I.4.3:

For $Z_0 := Z_v(k,0)$ we obtain because of $x_k = x_v(Z_0)$ (compare i) and ii) in the proof of Lemma I.4.1)

$$\begin{aligned} f_\epsilon(Z_0) &= \frac{w-k}{1-\beta} + \frac{\beta}{1-\beta}\left[\left(\frac{w}{1-\beta} - Z_0\right)(1-G_\epsilon(x_k)) \right.\\ &\quad \left. + \frac{1}{1-\beta}\int_{x_k}^{\overline{x}+\epsilon} v(x)dG_\epsilon(x)\right] \\ &= \frac{w-k}{1-\beta} + \frac{\beta}{1-\beta}\left[k(1-G_\epsilon(x_k)) + \frac{1}{1-\beta}\int_{x_k}^{\overline{x}+\epsilon} v(x)dG_\epsilon(x)\right] \\ &= Z_0 - \frac{\beta}{1-\beta}kG_\epsilon(x_k) + \frac{\beta}{(1-\beta)^2}\int_{x_k}^{\overline{x}+\epsilon} v(x)dG_\epsilon(x) \\ &= Z_0 + \frac{\beta}{(1-\beta)^2}\int_{\overline{x}-\epsilon}^{\overline{x}+\epsilon} h_v(k,x)dG_\epsilon(x). \end{aligned}$$

Q.E.D.

Proof of Lemma I.4.4:

We must show three parts i), ii) and iii):

i) $K(\epsilon)$ is uniquely defined, for each $\epsilon > 0$:[1]

For each $\epsilon > 0$ we have $H(0,\epsilon) > 0$ and $H(k,\epsilon) < 0$ with $\hat{k} := -(1/(1-\beta))v(\overline{x}-\epsilon)$. Because of the continuity of $H(\cdot,\epsilon)$ there exists at least one $K(\epsilon)$ between $\hat{k}$ and 0 such that $H(K(\epsilon),\epsilon) = 0$. Since the partial derivative $\frac{\partial H(k,\epsilon)}{\partial k} = -(1-\beta)(G(x_k) - G(\overline{x}-\epsilon))$ is negative, it follows that there exists exactly one such $K(\epsilon)$.

[1] We omit here the index "v".

ii) $K(\cdot)$ is increasing for all $\epsilon > 0$.

By the Implicit Function Theorem $K(\cdot)$ is differentiable for $\epsilon > 0$. For these $\epsilon > 0$ $K(\epsilon)$ is determined by the equation

$$K(\epsilon)(1-\beta)(G(x_{K\epsilon})) - G(\overline{x}-\epsilon)) = \int_{x_{k(\epsilon)}}^{\overline{x}+\epsilon} v(x)dx$$

therefore we get by differentiating both sides of this equation

$$K'(\epsilon) = (v(\overline{x}+\epsilon) - K(\epsilon)(1-\beta))/[(1-\beta)(G(x_{K(\epsilon)}) - G(\overline{x}-\epsilon))];$$

here use is made of (55): $v(x_{K(\epsilon)}) = -K(\epsilon)(1-\beta)$. Since $K(\epsilon) < \hat{k}$, it follows that $x_{K(\epsilon)} > \overline{x} - \epsilon$. Consequently it remains to show that the inequality $(v(\overline{x}+\epsilon) - K(\epsilon)(1-\beta)) > 0$ is valid.[2]

For this sake we consider the set of pairs $(\epsilon, K) \in \mathbf{R}^2$ satisfying the equation

$$v(\overline{x}+\epsilon) - K(1-\beta) = 0.$$

According to the Implicit Function Theorem by this equation there is defined a function $\tilde{K}(\cdot)$ given by

$$\tilde{K}(\epsilon) = \frac{v(\overline{x}+\epsilon)}{1-\beta}.$$

Obviously $\tilde{K}'(\epsilon) > 0$ and $\tilde{K}(0) = 0$. As it will be demonstrated below we have $K(0) = 0$. Now let us suppose $K'(0) < 0$; this would imply

$$(v(\overline{x}+\epsilon) - K(\epsilon)(1-\beta)) < 0$$

for ϵ near zero, and consequently $K(\epsilon) > \tilde{K}(\epsilon)$. As $\tilde{K}(\cdot)$ is strictly increasing in ϵ this is a contradiction. Now let us suppose that $K'(\epsilon') < 0$ for some $\epsilon' > 0$. Then there must be an $0 < \tilde{\epsilon} < \epsilon'$ such that $K'(\tilde{\epsilon}) = 0$ and[3] $K(\tilde{\epsilon}) = \tilde{K}(\tilde{\epsilon})$. Furthermore we have $K(\epsilon') > \tilde{K}(\epsilon')$ in contrast to $\tilde{K}'(\cdot) > 0$.

iii) $\lim_{\epsilon \downarrow 0} K(\epsilon) = 0$:

Using l'Hospital's rule we get: $\lim_{\epsilon\downarrow 0} H(k,\epsilon) = (1/2)$.

$$\lim_{\epsilon\downarrow 0} \frac{\partial \tilde{H}(k,\epsilon)}{\partial \epsilon} = -(1/2)k(1-\beta),$$

since $v(\overline{x}) = 0$; here we have defined

$$\tilde{H}(k,\epsilon) := -k(1-\beta)(x_k - \overline{x} + \epsilon) + \int_{x_k}^{\overline{x}+\epsilon} v(x)dx,$$

such that $H(k,\epsilon) = (1/2\epsilon)\tilde{H}(k,\epsilon)$. This implies $\lim_{\epsilon\downarrow 0} H(0,\epsilon) = 0$, and therefore we get the desired relation. Q.E.D.

---

[2] We define $x(\tilde{K}(\epsilon)) := x_{K(\epsilon)}$, to make the relevant dependencies transparent.

[3] ϵ is supposed to be the nearest local maximum of $K(\cdot)$ below ϵ'.

Proof of Proposition I.4.4:

We define $g : \mathbf{R}_+^2 \to \mathbf{R}$ by

$$g(k,\alpha) := -k(1-\beta)(\tilde{x}(k,\alpha) - \overline{x} + \epsilon) + \int_{\tilde{x}(k,\alpha)}^{\overline{x}+\epsilon} v(x,\alpha)dx$$

where $\tilde{x}(k,\alpha)$ is given by: $v(\tilde{x}(k,\alpha),\alpha) = -k(1-\beta)$.

Then $K(\epsilon,\alpha)$ is the solution of $g(\cdot,\alpha) = 0$. Since $\frac{\partial g(k,\alpha)}{\partial k} < 0$, the sign of $\frac{\partial K(\epsilon,\alpha)}{\partial \alpha}$ is thus equal to the sign of $\frac{\partial g(k,\alpha)}{\partial \alpha}$, by the Implicit Function Theorem. Now

$$\frac{\partial g(k,\alpha)}{\partial \alpha} = \int_{x(\tilde{k},\alpha)}^{\overline{x}+\epsilon} \frac{\partial v(x,\alpha)}{\partial \alpha} dx,$$

and thus the assertion follows from (60). Q.E.D.

Appendix A.II

Proof of Proposition II.3.1:

Without loss of generality we may assume $\beta = 1$. Furthermore we will use here the following convention

$$c := c_1, \quad c^*(\cdot) = c_1^*(\cdot), \quad y := y_1, \quad w := y_2, \quad r := r_2.$$

We will prove the proposition concerning the explicit shape of the (y, w)–section

$$R_2^*(y,w) = \{(\eta, q) \in \mathbf{R}_+ \times \mathbf{R}_{++} | \eta(y - qc^*(q)) \geq (y - qc^*(q)) + w/r\}$$

of the remigration set R_2^* in several steps. A good deal of work will be done if we know qualitative features of the function

$$g(q) := qc^*(q), \tag{1}$$

where $c^*(q)$ is given by

$$V_1(s) = U(q, c^*(q)) := \max_c \{u_1(c) + \int V_2(\cdot, r(y - qc), 2) d\varphi_1(\cdot|z)\} \tag{2}$$

for $s = (z, 0, 2) = (\Pi, p_1, q, y, 0, 2)$.

In the first lemma below relevant information about the explicit form of the function $U(\cdot, \cdot)$ with

$$U(q,c) = u_1(c) + \int V_2(\cdot, r(y - pc), 2) d\varphi_1(\cdot|z) \tag{3}$$

is given.

Lemma 1: *Given an arbitrary $q > 0$, we have*

$$U(q,c) = \left[\begin{array}{ll} -\infty, & \textit{for} \quad c \leq b \quad \textit{and} \quad c \geq c_q \\ \ln(c - b) + \ln(w + r(y - qc)) + 1/\Psi(qc) + I & \textit{for} \quad c \in (b, y/q) \\ \ln(c - b) + \ln(w + r(y - qc)) + I & \textit{for} \quad c \in [y/q, c_q), \end{array} \right. \tag{4}$$

where

$$\Psi(qc) := (w/r)/(y - qc) + 1 \quad \textit{for} \quad c < y/q \tag{5}$$

$$c_q \textit{ is given by } \quad w + r(y - qc_q) = 0 \tag{6}$$

$$I \textit{ is an expression independent of } q \textit{ and } c \tag{7}$$

Proof:

i) $c \leq b$: We have $u_1(c) = -\infty$, the result follows immediately.

ii) $c \geq c_q$: Since c_q is the maximum period–1–consumption, such that non-negative period–2–consumption is admissible, it follows that for $c \geq c_q$ period–2–utility is $= -\infty$, and therefore the result holds.

iii) $c \in [y/q, c_q)$: For such (q,c) the set

$$D(q,c) := \{(\Pi_2, p_{12}, p_{22}) | (\Pi_2 r/p_{12})(y - qc) \geq [(y - qc)r + w]/p_{22}\} \quad (8)$$

is empty. Thus we have

$$V_2(z_2, y - pc, 2) = u_2(((y - qc)r + w)/p_{22}) = \ln((y - qc)r + w) - \ln p_{22}$$

and the desired result holds too.

(iv) $c \in (b, y/q)$: Here we have

$$V_2(\Pi_2, p_{12}, p_{22}, w, y - qc, 2) = \max\{u_2((r\Pi_2/p_{12})(y - qc)),$$

$$u_2(((y - qc)r + w)/p_{22})\} = \max\{\ln(r\Pi_2/p_{12}) + \ln(y - qc), \ln((y - qc)r + w) - \ln p_{22}\},$$

and therefore we obtain

$$\begin{aligned} U(q,c) &= \ln(c - b) + \ln(y - qc)\varphi_1(D(q,c)) + \int_{D(q,c)} \ln(r\Pi_2/p_{12}) d\varphi_1 \\ &+ \ln((y - qc)r + w)(1 - \varphi_1(D(q,c)) - \int_{D'(q,c)} \ln(p_{22}) d\varphi_1, \end{aligned}$$

where $D'(\cdot)$ denotes the complement of $D(\cdot)$. From assumption (A.2) in II.3. and (8) we substitute

$$\varphi_1(D(q,c)) = 1 - H(\Psi(qc)) = 1/\Psi(qc)$$

and

$$\begin{aligned} \int_{D(q,c)} \ln(r\Pi_2/p_{12}) d\varphi_1 - \int_{D'(q,c)} \ln p_{22}\, d\varphi_1 &= \int_{D(q,c)} \ln(r\eta) dH(\eta) - \int \ln(p_{22}) d\varphi_1 \\ &= \int_{\Psi(qc)}^{\infty} \ln(r\eta) dH(\eta) + I \\ &= \ln(r\Psi(qc)) \frac{1}{\Psi(qc)} + 1/\Psi(qc) + I \end{aligned}$$

which gives the desired result after some tedious calculations. Q.E.D.

It follows from Lemma 1 that

$$c^*(q) = \arg\max U(q,c)$$

is contained in the interval (b, c_q). Without loss of generality we can omit the term I if we are looking for qualitative features of $c^*(q)$ and $g(q) = qc^*(q)$. We denote the modified function $U(q,c) - I$ again by $U(q,c)$.

Furthermore we define

$$\underline{c}(q) := \arg\max\{U(q,c); b < c < y/q\}$$

and

$$\overline{c}(q) := \arg\max\{U(q,c); y/q \le c < c_q\}.$$

Obviously $c^*(q)$ is either equal to $\underline{c}(q)$ or to $\overline{c}(q)$. More information about the position of $c^*(q)$ is given by the next Lemma.

Lemma 2: *We have*

$$c^*(q) = \left[\begin{array}{lll} \underline{c}(q) & \textit{for} & q \le q_0 := 1/b(y - w/r) \\ \overline{c}(q) & \textit{for} & q \ge q_1 := 1/b(y - w/2r) \end{array} \right.$$

Proof:

i) $q \le q_0$:

a) For $c \in (b, y/q)$ we have

$$\underline{u}(q,c) := \frac{\partial U}{\partial c} = \frac{1}{c-b} - \frac{rq}{w + r(y - qc)} - \frac{rqw}{(w + r(y - cq))^2}$$

Obviously $\underline{u}(q,\cdot)$ is strictly decreasing in c with $\lim_{c \to b} \underline{u}(q,c) = +\infty$ and $\lim_{c \to y} \underline{u}(q,c) = q/(y - qb) - 2qr/w < 0$ (even for $q < q_1$). Thus $\underline{c}(q)$ exists and is the solution of $\underline{u}(q,c) = 0$.

b) For $c \in [y/q, c_q]$ we have

$$\overline{u}(q,c) := \frac{\partial U}{\partial c} = \frac{1}{c-b} - \frac{rq}{w + (y - qc)r}.$$

Since $\overline{u}(q,\cdot)$ is strictly decreasing in c, too, and non-positive for $y \le q_0$ at $c = y/q$, we must have: $\overline{c}(q) = y/q$.

a) and b) together yield: $c^*(q) = \underline{c}(q)$ for $q \le q_0$, and $c^*(q)$ is the solution of $\underline{u}(q,c) = 0$.

This result is illustrated by the following drawing

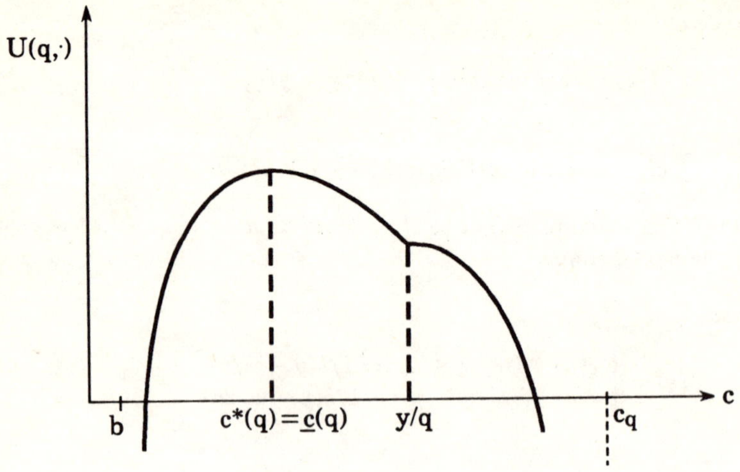

Figure 15: Graph of $U(q,\cdot)$ in case (i)

ii) $q \geq q_1$: One can easily see that $\overline{u}(q, y/q) > 0$ even for $q > q_0$, $\lim_{c \to c_q} \overline{u}(q, c) = -\infty$ and $\underline{u}(q, c) > 0$ for $c \in (b, y/q)$. Consequently we have $c^*(q) = \overline{c}(q)$ and $c^*(q)$ is the unique solution of the equation $\overline{u}(q, c) = 0$.

We can illustrate this result by the drawing below:

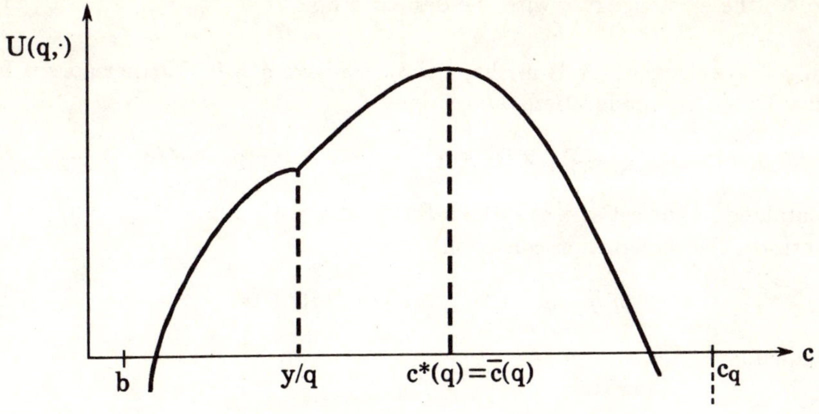

Figure 16: Graph of $U(q,\cdot)$ in case (ii)

Q.E.D.

Now we use a continuity argument to show

Lemma 3: *There exists a unique price* $\hat{q} \in (q_0, q_1)$ *characterized by* $U(\hat{q}, \underline{c}(\hat{q})) = U(\hat{q}, \overline{c}(\hat{q}))$ *such that*

$$c^*(q) = \left[\begin{array}{lll} \underline{c}(q) & \mathit{for} & q < \hat{q} \\ \overline{c}(q) & \mathit{for} & q > \hat{q} \end{array} \right.$$

Proof: It follows from Lemma 2 that

$$\begin{array}{lll} U(q,\underline{c}(q)) > U(q,\overline{c}(q)) & \text{for} \quad q \le q_0 & \text{and} \\ U(q,\underline{c}(q)) < U(q,\overline{c}(q)) & \text{for} \quad q \ge q_1. & \end{array}$$

Furthermore it has been shown in the proof of Lemma 2 that $\underline{c}(q)$ (resp. $\overline{c}(q)$) is the solution of $\underline{u}(q,c) = 0$ (resp. of $\overline{u}(q,c) = 0$) even for $q < q_1$ (resp. for $q > q_0$).

Therefore we have for $q \in (q_0, q_1)$:

$$\frac{dU(q,\underline{c}(q))}{dq} = \frac{\partial U(q,\underline{c}(q))}{\partial q} = \frac{1}{q}\frac{\underline{c}(q)}{b - \underline{c}(q)} < \frac{1}{q}\frac{\overline{c}(q)}{b - \overline{c}(q)} = \frac{\partial U(q,\overline{c}(q))}{\partial q} = \frac{U(q,\overline{c}(q))}{dq}$$

(where the equations $\underline{u}(q,\underline{c}(q)) = 0$ and $\overline{u}(q,\overline{c}(q)) = 0$ are utilized).

This proves the existence of $\hat{q}$ with the desired properties. Q.E.D.

Since $q_0 > 0$ (because of (A.3) in chap. II.3), we have $\hat{q} > 0$. Furthermore it follows from Lemma 3 that the remigration–set–section

$$R_2^*(y,w) = \{(\eta,q) \in \mathbf{R}_+ \times \mathbf{R}_{++} | \eta r(y - qc^*(q)) \geq r(y - qc^*(q)) + w\}$$

must be contained in the set $\{(\eta,q) \in \mathbf{R}_+ \times \mathbf{R}_{++} | 0 < q < \hat{q}\}$. Since $c^*(q) < y/q$ for $q < \hat{q}$ we can transform the remigration condition

$$\eta(y - qc^*(q))r \geq r(y - qc^*(q)) + w$$

into the inequality

$$\eta \geq f(q)$$

with $f : (0,\hat{q}) \to \mathbf{R}$ defined by

$$f(q) := \Psi(qc^*(q)) \underset{(1)}{=} \Psi(g(q)) \tag{9}$$

where Ψ is given by (5) in Lemma 1.

The properties of f are demonstrated by the following Lemma

Lemma 4: *The function f is*

(i) strictly increasing

(ii) strictly convex

(iii) bounded below by 1.

Proof:

(i) Obviously we have

$$\frac{df(q)}{dq} = \frac{d\Psi(g)}{dg}\frac{dg(q)}{dq} \quad \text{and} \quad \frac{d\Psi}{dg} > 0.$$

Consequently it remains to show $\frac{dg}{dq} > 0$. By definition $g(q)$ solves the equation

$$\frac{1}{g(q) - qb} = \frac{r}{w + (y - g(q))r} + \frac{rw}{(w + (y - g(q))r)^2} \tag{10}$$

By differentiation we obtain

$$\frac{dg(q)}{dq}\left[\frac{1}{(g(q) - qb)^2} + \frac{r^2}{a^2} + \frac{2r^2w}{a^3}\right] = \frac{b}{(g(q) - qb)^2}$$

where $a := w + (y - g(q))r > 0$, which gives the desired result.

(ii) One can show by some transformations[4] that $\frac{d^2 g(q)}{dq^2} \geq 0$; consequently one obtains

$$\frac{d^2 f(q)}{dq^2} = \frac{d^2 \Psi(g)}{dg^2} (\frac{dg(q))}{dq})^2 + \frac{d\Psi(g)}{dg} \frac{d^2 g(q)}{dq^2} > 0$$

because of $\frac{d^2 \Psi}{dg^2} > 0$; thus f is strictly convex.

(iii) follows from the definition of $\Psi(\cdot)$ together with $w > 0$ and $y - g(q) > 0$. Q.E.D.

Proof of Proposition II.3.2:

Expressing the explicit dependence of $c^*(q)$ on y and w by writing g, given by (1), as $g(q, y, w) = qc^*(q, y, w)$ we obtain by differentiating f w.r.t. y resp. w; (compare (9) and (5)):

$$\frac{\partial f}{\partial y} = (w/r) \frac{\frac{\partial g}{\partial y} - 1}{(y - g(q, y, w))^2} \tag{11}$$

$$\frac{\partial f}{\partial w} = (1/r) \frac{y - g(q, y, w) + w \frac{\partial g}{\partial w}}{(y - g(q, y, w))^2} \tag{12}$$

Now utilizing equation (10) in the proof of Lemma 4 we have by differentiating (10) with respect to y and to w

$$\frac{-\frac{\partial g}{\partial y}}{(g - qb)^2} = r^2 (\frac{\partial g}{\partial y} - 1) \left(\frac{1}{a^2} + \frac{2w}{a^3} \right) \tag{13}$$

$$\frac{\partial g}{\partial w} \left(\frac{1}{(g - qb)^2} + \frac{r^2}{a^2} + \frac{2r^2 w}{a^3} \right) = \frac{r}{a^2}. \tag{14}$$

From (13) we can conclude $\frac{\partial g}{\partial y} \in (0, 1)$ which implies $\frac{\partial f}{\partial y} < 0$ by (11). From the second equation we conclude $\frac{\partial g}{\partial w} > 0$, implying $\frac{\partial f}{\partial w} > 0$. - These qualitative properties of f demonstrate the variation of $R_2^*(y_1, y_2)$ as asserted in the Proposition. Q.E.D.

[4] $g(q)$ can be calculated explicitly from (9) as the solution of a square equation, that is given by $g(q) =$ "linear function in $q - 1/4\sqrt{d(q)}$", where $d(q) := [r(y - qb) + 4w] - 8w^2$; then it can be demonstrated that $\sqrt{d(\cdot)}$ is a concave function in q.

Appendix A.III

Part A: Technical Results

Lemma A.1: *Suppose assumptions (A.1)-(A.3) are valid then the supply functions* $S_{it}(\underline{w}_{t-1}, \underline{x}_t(\cdot), \cdot) : \mathbf{R}^2_+ \rightarrow \mathbf{R}_+$ *are continuous.*

Proof: According to the definition of $S_{it}(\cdot)$ we have to show that the functions $M_{it}(\cdot)$ and $R_i(\underline{w}_{t-1}, x_{jt}(\cdot), \cdot)$ are continuous in $\underline{w}_t$.

1. Let us define the sets $\{A_n\}$ as follows

$$A_n := \{l_i \in L_i | E_i(\underline{w}^n, l_i) > 0\}.$$

Then we obtain

$$M_{it}(\underline{w}^n) = \lambda(\{A_n\}) = \int \underline{1}_{A_n} d\lambda.$$

Now let us consider a sequence of wages $\{\underline{w}_t^n\}_n$ converging to $\underline{w}_t^o$. We want to derive the implication

$$(\underline{w}_t^n \rightarrow \underline{w}_t^o) \Rightarrow (\underline{1}_{A_n}(\cdot) \rightarrow 1_{A_o}(\cdot)) \quad \lambda - \text{a.e.} \quad (n \rightarrow \infty) \tag{1}$$

From (1) continuity of $M_{it}(\cdot)$ easily follows from the dominated convergence theorem.

To prove the validity of (1) we will argue as follows:

Let us suppose for the moment that $E_i(\cdot, l_i)$ is continuous in $\underline{w}_t$. Now let us consider agents l_i', l_i'' with[5]

$$\begin{aligned} E_i(\underline{w}_o, l_i') &> 0 \quad \text{and} \\ E_i(\underline{w}_o, l_i'') &< 0. \end{aligned}$$

Then we have $l_i' \in A_o$, $l_i'' \notin A_o$ and because of the continuity of $E_i(\cdot, l_i)$ we can conclude

$$\begin{aligned} \underline{1}_{A_n}(l_i') &\rightarrow \underline{1}_{A_o}(l_i') \quad \text{and} \\ \underline{1}_{A_n}(l_i'') &\rightarrow \underline{1}_{A_o}(l_i''). \end{aligned}$$

A problem in convergence of the indicator–functions $\underline{1}_{A_n}(\cdot)$ could arise only for the set

$$M_o := \{l_i \in L_i | E_i(\underline{w}_o, l_i) = 0\}.$$

According to (A.4) we have $\lambda(\{M_o\}) = 0$ implying the validity of (1). It remains to show the continuity of $E_i(\cdot, l_i)$ for arbitrary $l_i \in L_i$. It follows from the definition of $E_i(\underline{w}, l_i)$ that the only problem in continuity could arise for the integral

$$\int_{K(\underline{w}) \times X} \max\{w_j' + x_j - w_i', 0\} d\varphi_{l_i}(\underline{w}', x_j | \underline{w}^o).$$

[5]Here and in the sequel we define
$E_i(\underline{w}_t^*, l) = E_i(\underline{w}_t^*, \varphi_i(\underline{w}_t^* | l))$

Let us consider a sequence of wage rates $\{\underline{w}^n\}_n$ with $\underline{w}^n \to \underline{w}^o$ then we have

$$\int_{K(\underline{w}^n)\times X} \max\{\cdot\} d\varphi_{l_i}(\cdot|\underline{w}^n) \to \int_{K(\underline{w}^o)\times X} \max\{\cdot\} d\varphi_{l_i}(\cdot|\underline{w}^o).$$

This follows from the continuity of $\varphi_{l_i}(\cdot|\cdot)$ in $\underline{w}$ and from the definition of $K(\underline{w}^n)$ (see (A.1)). For n large enough we can substitute the sets $K(\underline{w}^n)$ by a common compact set K containing $K(\underline{w}^n)$ $\forall \underline{w}^n$ $(n \geq n')$ and obtain the result from the definition of weak convergence.

2. Now let us define the sets

$$\begin{aligned} A &:= \{l_i \in L_i | E_i(\underline{w}_{t-1}, l_i) > 0\}, \\ B_n &:= \{l_i \in L_i | D_i(\underline{w}_t^n, x_{jt}(l_i)) > 0\}, \\ C_n &= A \cap B_n. \end{aligned}$$

Then we have to show (analogously as before)

$$(\underline{w}_t^n \to \underline{w}_t^o) \Rightarrow 1_{C_n}(\cdot) \to 1_{C_o}(\cdot) \quad \lambda-\text{a.e.} \quad (n \to \infty) \tag{2}$$

To show the validity of (2) we can argue similarly as above: $D_i(\cdot, x_{jt}(l_i))$ is trivially continuous in $\underline{w}_t$ and $\lambda(\{N_o\}) = 0$ (because of (A.4)), where

$$N_o := \{l_i \in L_i | E_i(\underline{w}_{t-1}, l_i) > 0 \quad \text{and} \quad D_i(\underline{w}_t, x_{jt}(l_i)) = 0\}$$

Consequently we obtain the desired continuity of $R_{it}(\cdot)$.

Q.E.D.

Proof of Proposition III.3.1:

We define a function

$$H(\underline{w}_{t-1}, \underline{x}_t(\cdot), \cdot) : Z^2 \to Z^2,$$

where $Z := [0, 2n_i + 2n_j]$, as follows

$$\begin{aligned} H(\underline{w}_{t-1}, \underline{x}_t(\cdot), (s_1, s_2)) \;:=\; & (S_1(\underline{w}_{t-1}, \underline{x}_t(\cdot), f_1(s_1), f_2(s_2)), \\ & S_2(\underline{w}_{t-1}, \underline{x}_t(\cdot), f_1(s_1), f_2(s_2))). \end{aligned}$$

According to Lemma A.1 the functions $S_i(\underline{w}_{t-1}, \underline{x}_t(\cdot), \cdot)$ are continuous in $\underline{w}_t$. As Z^2 is a compact and convex set we can apply Brouwer's fixed-point theorem to the mapping $H(\underline{w}_{t-1}, \underline{x}_t(\cdot), \cdot)$. Let (s_1^*, s_2^*) denote the fixed point of $H(\cdot)$, then the equilibrium wage rate $\underline{w}_i^*$ obviously is given by $w_i^* = f_i(s_i^*)$. Q.E.D.

Proof of Lemma III.3.1:

1) Because of $w_{it} = w_{jt}, \varphi_i(\underline{w}_t|l_i) = \varphi_j(\underline{w}_t|l_j)$ for $l_i = l_j$ and $L_{it} = L_{jt}$ we have

$$\{l_i \in L_{it}|E_i(\underline{w}_t, \varphi_i(l_i)) > 0\} = \{l_j \in L_{jt}|E_j(\underline{w}_t, \varphi_j(l_j)) > 0\},$$

which implies $M_{it}(\underline{w}_t) = M_{jt}(\underline{w}_t)$. By inserting $\underline{w}_t$ with $w_{1t} = w_{2t}$ into $E_i(\cdot)$ we can conclude from (A.6) that $M_{it}(\underline{w}_t) > 0$.

2) Because of the assumption $w_{it-1} = w_{jt-1}$ we can conclude analogously as above that

$$\{l_i \in L_{it-1}|E_i(\underline{w}_{t-1}, \varphi_i(l_i) > 0\} = \{l_j \in L_{jt-1}|E_j(\underline{w}_{t-1}, \varphi_j(l_j) > 0\}.$$

Similarly we obtain

$$\{l_i \in L_{it-1}|D_i(\underline{w}_t, x_{jt}(l_i)) > 0\} = \{l_j \in L_{jt-1}|D_j(\underline{w}_t, x_{it}(l_j)) > 0\}$$

which implies

$$R_{it}(\underline{w}_{t-1}, x_{jt}(\cdot), \underline{w}_t) = R_{jt}(\underline{w}_{t-1}, x_{it}(\cdot), \underline{w}_t).$$

Q.E.D.

Proof of Proposition III.3.2:

We consider the set of all symmetric equilibrium candidates, that is, the diagonal in $\mathbf{R}^2_+$.

For such wage profiles we conclude from lemma III.3.1

$$S_i(\underline{w}_{t-1}, \underline{x}_t(\cdot), (w, w)) = S_j(\underline{w}_{t-1}, \underline{x}_t(\cdot), (w, w)),$$

which implies $S_i(\cdot, (w, w)) = S_j(\cdot, (w, w)) = n_{t-1} + n_t$ ($n_{it-1} = n_{jt-1} = n_{t-1}$ and $n_{it} = n_{jt} = n_t$). Then we set $w^* = f_i(n_{t-1} + n_t) = f_j(n_{t-1} + n_t)$ (> 0). Obviously $w^* = (w^*, w^*)$ is the unique symmetric equilibrium. Q.E.D.

Proof of Proposition III.3.3.:

1) Suppose $\underline{w}_t^*$ is an equilibrium with $w_{1t}^* = w_{2t}^*$. Then we can conclude from the arguments in lemma III.3.1

$$R_1(\underline{w}_{t-1}, x_{2t}(\cdot), \underline{w}_t^*) = R_2(\underline{w}_{t-1}, x_{1t}(\cdot), \underline{w}_t^*).$$

Furthermore it follows from the definition of an equilibrium

$$f_1(S_1(\underline{w}_{t-1}, \underline{x}_t(\cdot), \underline{w}_t^*)) = f_2(S_2(\underline{w}_{t-1}, \underline{x}_t(\cdot), \underline{w}_t^*))$$

which implies

$$M_2(\underline{w}_t^*) - M_1(\underline{w}_t^*) = R_1(\cdot, \underline{w}_t^*) - R_2(\cdot, \underline{w}_t^*) = 0$$

and finally

$$M_1(\underline{w}_t^*) = M_2(\underline{w}_t^*). \tag{1}$$

Now let us consider the inequality

$$\begin{aligned} E_1(\underline{w}_t^*, l) &= \int \max\{x_{2t+1}, 0\} dv_l(x_{2t+1}) \\ > E_2(\underline{w}_t^*, l) &= \int \max\{x_{1t+1}, 0\} dv_l(x_{1t+1}) \end{aligned}$$

which follows from (A.7) together with the "MPS"–assumption (*) in the theorem (as the integrand is a convex function, see Lippman/McCall (1982)). From (A.8) we obtain the relation

$$\{l \in L_{1t} | E_1(\underline{w}_t^*, l) > 0\} \supsetneqq \{l \in L_{2t} | E_2(\underline{w}_t^*, l) > 0\}$$

which implies

$$M_{1t}(\underline{w}_t^*) > M_{2t}(\underline{w}_t^*),$$

a contradiction to (1).

2) Now let us suppose $\underline{w}_t^*$ is a migration equilibrium with $w_{1t}^* < w_{2t}^*$. Then we obtain immediately from the "identical country" assumption

$$R_{1t}(\underline{w}_{t-1}, x_{2t}(\cdot), \underline{w}_t^*) \leq R_{2t}(\underline{w}_{t-1}, x_{1t}(\cdot), \underline{w}_t^*).$$

From the definition of an equilibrium follow the inequalities

$$f_1(S_{1t}(\ldots)) < f_2(S_{2t}(\ldots)),$$

$$\begin{aligned} -M_{1t}(\underline{w}_t^*) + M_{2t}(\underline{w}_t^*) + R_{1t}(\underline{w}_{t-1}, x_{2t}(\cdot), \underline{w}_t^*) - R_{2t}(\underline{w}_{t-1}, x_{1t}(\cdot), \underline{w}_t^*) \\ > \; -M_{2t}(\underline{w}_t^*) + M_{1t}(\underline{w}_t^*) + R_{2t}(\underline{w}_{t-1}, x_{1t}(\cdot), \underline{w}_t^*) - R_{1t}(\underline{w}_{t-1}, x_{2t}(\cdot), \underline{w}_t^*) \end{aligned}$$

and

$$M_{2t}(\underline{w}_t^*) - M_{1t}(\underline{w}_t^*) > R_{2t}(\underline{w}_{t-1}, x_{1t}(\cdot), \underline{w}_t^*) - R_{1t}(\underline{w}_{t-1}, x_{2t}(\cdot), \underline{w}_t^*),$$

and finally

$$M_{2t}(\underline{w}_t^*) > M_{1t}(\underline{w}_t^*). \tag{2}$$

But from an analogous consideration as above we obtain

$$\begin{aligned} \{l \in L_{1t} | w_{2t}^* - w_{1t}^* &> -\int \max\{w_{2t}^* - w_{1t}^* + x_{2t+1}, 0\} dv_l\} \\ &\supset \{l \in L_{2t} | w_{1t}^* - w_{2t}^* - \\ &\quad \int \max\{w_{1t}^* - w_{2t}^* + x_{1t+1}, 0\} dv_l\} \end{aligned} \tag{3}$$

which implies $M_{1t}(\underline{w}_t^*) \geq M_{2t}(\underline{w}_t^*)$, in contradiction to (2).

To prove relation (3) we establish the following set of inequalities for agents l contained in the right–hand set of (3):

$$\begin{aligned} -\int \max\{w^*_{2t} - w^*_{1t} + x_{2t+1}, 0\} dv_l &< -\int \max\{w^*_{2t} - w^*_{1t} + x_{1t+1}, 0\} dv_l \qquad (4)\\ &\leq -\int \max\{w^*_{1t} - w^*_{2t} + x_{1t+1}, 0\} dvl \\ &< w^*_{1t} - w^*_{2t} \end{aligned}$$

where the first inequality follows from the "MPS–assumption" (*) and the third inequality from the definition of the right–hand set in (3). The second inequality follows from our hypothesis $w^*_{1t} < w^*_{2t}$.

Finally, from this hypothesis together with (4) we can derive the inequality

$$-\int \max\{w^*_{2t} - w^*_{1t} + x_{2t+1}, 0\} dv_l < w^*_{1t} - w^*_{2t} < w^*_{2t} - w^*_{1t},$$

which implies the validity of relation (3).

3) From (1) and (2) we can conclude that for an equilibrium wage rate we must have

$$w^*_{1t} > w^*_{2t},$$

which implies $R_{1t}(\underline{w}_{t-1}, x_{2t}(\cdot), \underline{w}^*_t) \geq R_{2t}(\underline{w}_{t-1}, x_{1t}(\cdot), \underline{w}^*_t)$. As we have in equilibrium

$$f_1(S_{1t}(\cdot)) > f_2(S_{2t}(\cdot)),$$

the following inequalities can be derived

$$\begin{aligned} &-M_{1t}(\underline{w}^*_t) + M_{2t}(\underline{w}^*_t) + R_{1t}(\underline{w}_{t-1}, x_{2t+1}(\cdot), \underline{w}^*_t) - R_2(\underline{w}_{t-1}, x_{1t+1}(\cdot), \underline{w}^*_t) \\ &\quad < \; -M_{2t}(\underline{w}^*_t) + M_{1t}(\underline{w}^*_t) - R_{1t}(\underline{w}_{t-1}, x_{2t+1}(\cdot), \underline{w}^*_t) + R_{2t}(\underline{w}_{t-1}, x_{1t+1}(\cdot), \underline{w}^*_t), \end{aligned}$$

$$M_{1t}(\underline{w}^*_t) - M_{2t}(\underline{w}^*_t) > R_{1t}(\underline{w}_t, x_{2t+1}(\cdot), \underline{w}^*_t) - R_{2t}(\underline{w}_{t-1}, x_{1t}(\cdot), \underline{w}^*_t) \geq 0,$$

$$M_{1t}(\underline{w}^*_t) > M_{2t}(\underline{w}^*_t).$$

Q.E.D.

Appendix A.III

Part B: Some Remarks Concerning Assumption (A.4)

It is the purpose of the present part of the appendix to establish sufficient conditions that guarantee the validity of assumption (A.4). This seems to be useful as it is not easy to see by mere introspection how (A.4) could be satisfied in an arbitrarily given model.

We will concentrate here on the first part of (A.4) only, where it is stated that for all $\underline{w}$ the set of agents[6]

$$L_o(w) := \{l \in L | E(\underline{w}, \varphi(l)) = 0\}$$

is negligible, that is in technical terms, has Lebesgue–measure equal to zero (for the second part completely analogous considerations are applicable).

Our reasoning is motivated by the following observation: if all agents $l \in L$ are identical in the sense of having the same expectation function $\varphi(l)$, then we must expect that $L_o(\underline{w})$ is either equal to L or empty. But this would cause some serious discontinuity of the function $M_{it}(\cdot)$ – as given by (11) –, such that we cannot expect that the auctioneer is able to find an equilibrating wage profile $\underline{w}^*$. This phenomenon, which is an example of a well–known problem in economic equilibrium analysis, motivates us to postulate some kind of "heterogeneity" of the agents.

To simplify the notation and the technical complexity we restrict ourselves here to the following special version of our model: it is assumed that for each $\underline{w}$ the probability measure $\varphi(\underline{w}|l)$ can be split up as a product measure as follows

$$\varphi(\underline{w}|l) = \varphi^{(1)}(\underline{w}) \times \varphi^{(2)}(l)$$

where $\varphi^{(1)}(\underline{w})$ is a probability distribution over $(\mathbf{R}^2, B(\mathbf{R}^2))$ and $\varphi^{(2)}(l)$ denotes a probability distribution over $(X, B(X))$. I.e. we suppose that the forecasts about future wage rates and the quality of living can be made independently and furthermore that only the latter are 'agent–dependent' but do not depend on the prevailing wage profile $\underline{w}$. According to this assumption one can conclude that potential migrants are building the same wage expectations based on the past wage profile more or less objectively while the expectations about the quality of living are built subjectively and may differ from agent to agent.

Now we will show that the following heterogeneity assumption will be sufficient to guarantee the validity of the first part of (A.4).

(H) *For each $l \in L$ and each neighbourhood V of l in L there is a neighbourhood U of the probability measure $\varphi^{(2)}(l)$ of agent l in the set $M(X)$ of all probability distributions over X (endowed with the weak topology) such that U is contained in the image $\varphi^{(2)}(V)$.*

[6] We omit here and in the following the indices i and t.

This assumption roughly says: whenever we consider an agent $l \in L$ and a set V of agents near to l, then we can associate to each probability measure $\Pi \in M(X)$ which is not "too different" from $\varphi^{(2)}$ (with respect to the topology of weak convergence) an agent $l' \in V$ with subjective probability distribution $\varphi^{(2)}(l') = \Pi$. In other words, in (H) continuity of the inverse image correspondence $\varphi^{(2)-1}(\cdot)$ is postulated. Now we can prove the following lemma as the main result of this part of the appendix.

Lemma B.1.: *Suppose that (H) is satisfied, then the first part of assumption (A.4) is valid.*

Proof: Instead of the assertion of the lemma we shall even prove the following more general result:

(R.1) *(H) implies that for each bounded and continuous function $f : X \to \mathbf{R}$ and each real number c the set*

$$H(f;c) := \{l \in L | \int f(x) d\varphi^{(2)}(l)(x) = c\}$$

has Lebesgue–measure zero.

For the proof of (R.I) it is sufficient to show the validity of the following result:

(R.II) *For each $l \in H(f;c)$ and $\delta > 0$ there is some l' with $|l - l'| < \delta$ and $l' \notin H(f;c)$.*

Consider an $l \in H(f;c)$ and assume that there is some $\delta > 0$ such that the δ–neighbourhood of l in L is contained in $H(f;c)$. Then it follows by (H) that there is some neighbourhood U of $\varphi^{(2)}(l)$ in $M(X)$ such that U is even contained in the image of $H(f;c)$ under $\varphi^{(2)}$, and thus in the hyperplane

$$\{\Pi \in M(X)| \int f(x) d\Pi(x) = c\}.$$

But this is a contradiction, since that hyperplane has an empty interior. – Therefore (R.II), and by this (R.I) and the assertion of Lemma B.1 are shown to hold.

Q.E.D.

It is easy to see that postulate (H) essentially assures that the agents' subjective expectations about quality of life are sufficiently dispersed. In other words, agents in a neighbourhood of a given agent l do not stick to the same expectation function. We do not intend to stress the plausibility of this assumption too far. As we did not give an economic interpretation of the "neighbourhood of an agent $l \in L$" it would be difficult to judge the plausibility of assumption (H). Anyway, it does not seem to be counter–intuitive and furthermore, we think an assumption similar to (H) has to be made in all models where continuity of the aggregate response function of consumers confronted with binary choices plays a crucial role.

Appendix A.IV.2

Proof of Proposition IV.2.1:

We proceed in three steps:

1. Let $F(\cdot|\xi,\eta)$ denote the c.d.f. of a normal random variable with mean ξ and variance η independent of ξ. Then $F(\cdot|\xi,\eta)$ is stochastically increasing in ξ, i.e. for $\xi > \xi'$ we have
$$F(x|\xi,\eta) \leq F(x|\xi',\eta) \quad \text{for all} x.$$

2. For all $t = 1, \ldots, n_i^*$ the functions $B_t(\cdot)$ defined by (4) are increasing in x. This is shown by backward induction. Assume $B_{t+1}(\cdot)$ is increasing. Since
$$\begin{aligned} B_t(x) \quad := \quad & \alpha x + \beta \int \max\{\bar{y}^{(i)}_{1,t+1}, y^{(i)}_{2,t+1} \\ & + B_{t+1}(x')\} dF(x'|(1-\rho)\mu + \rho x, \sigma^2(1-\rho)), \end{aligned}$$
and since $\alpha > 0$, it suffices to show that the integral value is non–decreasing in x. Now by induction hypothesis the integrand $\max\{\ldots\}$ is non–decreasing in x', and therefore it follows from 1.[7] that the integral does not decrease for increasing x (since $\rho \leq 0$).

3. Since the optimality equation (6) shows that i will remigrate from 2 to 1 in period t iff $\bar{y}^{(i)}_{1t} \geq \bar{y}^{(i)}_{2t} + B_t(x)$, the assertions of Proposition IV.2.1 now follow immediately from 2.

Q.E.D.

7 Compare e.g. Theorem 1 in Lippman/McCall (1982).

Appendix A.IV.3

Proof of Prop. IV.3.1.

The state of information for $i \in I_{jt}$ is $((w_{jt}), (w_{ojt}))$. Then the Gittins index for the MAB–problem of i, for country j is according to our specific assumptions determined by

$$Z_{jt} = \frac{w_{jt}^*}{1-\beta} + \frac{\beta}{1-\beta}\left[\frac{w_{jt}^*}{1-\beta} - Z_{jt}\right]^+$$

from which we obtain

$$Z_{jt} = w_{jt}^*/(1-\beta). \tag{1}$$

The Gittins index of $i \in I_{jt}$ for country o is here determined by

$$\begin{aligned} Z_{ojt} &= \frac{w_{ojt}^* - k_{ojt}}{1-\beta} + \frac{\beta}{1-\beta}\left[\left(\frac{w_{ojt}^* - \overline{x}_{oj}}{1-\beta} - Z_{ojt}\right)^+ \cdot 1/2 \right. \\ &\left. + \left(\frac{w_{ojt}^* - \overline{x}_{oj}}{1-\beta} - Z_{ojt}\right)^+ \cdot 1/2\right] \end{aligned} \tag{2}$$

It can be checked that only

$$\text{either (a):} \quad \frac{w_{ojt}^* + \overline{x}_{oj}}{1-\beta} > Z_{ojt} > \frac{w_{ojt}^* - \overline{x}_{oj}}{1-\beta}$$

$$\text{or (b) :} \quad \frac{w_{ojt}^* + \overline{x}_{ojt}}{1-\beta} \geq Z_{ojt}$$

are possible as solutions of (2). From this we obtain

$$Z_{ojt} = \left[\begin{array}{ll} -\frac{k_{ojt}}{1-\beta} + \frac{w_{ojt}^*}{1-\beta} + \frac{(\beta/2)\overline{x}_{oj}}{(1-\beta)(1-\beta/2)}, & \text{in case (a)} \\ \frac{w_{ojt}^*}{1-\beta} - k_{ojt} & \text{in case (b).} \end{array}\right. \tag{3}$$

Thus (a) (rsp. (b)) holds, iff $k_{ojt} <$ (rsp. $\geq$) $x_{oj}/(1-\beta)$. According to Proposition I.3.1 we know that $i \in I_{jt}$ will migrate from j to o during period t iff $Z_{ojt} > Z_{jt}$. Therefore i will migrate from j to o during period t iff either $k_{ojt} < \overline{x}_{oj}/(1-\beta)$ and (22) hold, or $k_{ojt} \geq \overline{x}_{oj}/(1-\beta)$ and $k_{ojt} < (w_{ojt}^* - w_{jt}^*)/(1-\beta)$ hold. But by (21) the second case is excluded, thus the assertion of the proposition is proved. Q.E.D.

Proof of Prop. IV.3.2.

The state of information for $i \in I_{ojt}$ is according to the assumption (w_{ojt}, x_{ojt}) and $(w_{jt}, 0)$. Then it follows from Proposition I.3.2.

$$Z_{ojt} = \frac{w_{ojt}^* + x_{ojt}}{1-\beta} \quad \text{and} \quad Z_{jt} = \frac{w_{jt}^*}{1-\beta}.$$

Therefore the assertion of the proposition is an immediate consequence of Prop. I.3.1. Q.E.D.

List of References

BERNINGHAUS, S. (1984): Das "Multi-Armed-Bandit-Paradigma". A. Hain Meisenheim, Königstein/Ts.

BERNINGHAUS, S./SEIFERT-VOGT, H.G. (1987): International Migration under Incomplete Information. *Schweizerische Zeitschrift für Volkswirtschaft und Statistik* 2, 199–218.

BERNINGHAUS, S./SEIFERT-VOGT, H.G. (1988): Permanent vs. Temporary Migration – A Decision Theoretical Approach. *Journal of Population Economics* 1, 195–211.

BERNINGHAUS, S./SEIFERT-VOGT, H.G. (1989): *A Temporary Equilibrium Model for International Migration.* Disc.pap. No. 400–89, Universität Mannheim.

BLUME, L. (1979): The Ergodic Behaviour of Stochastic Processes of Economic Equilibria. *Econometrica* 47, 1421–1432.

BLUME, L. (1982): New Techniques for the Study of Stochastic Equilibrium Processes. *Journal of Mathematical Economics* 9, 61–70.

CEBULA, R.J. (1978): *The Determinants of Human Migration.* Heath Lexington Books.

GALOR, O. (1986): Time Preference and International Labour Migration. *Journal of Economic Theory* 38, 1–20.

GALOR, O./STARK, O. (1987): *The impact of differences in the levels of technology on international labour migration.* Disc.paper no. 34, Migration and Development Program, Harvard University.

GITTINS, J.C./JONES, D.M. (1974): A Dynamic Allocation Index for the Sequential Design of Experiments. In: *Progress in Statistics,* Gani ed., North–Holland, 241–266.

GITTINS, J.C./NASH, P. (1974): *Scheduling Queues and Dynamic Allocation Indices.* In: Proc. EMS, Prague, 191–202.

GITTINS, J.C. (1979): Bandit Processes and Dynamic Allocation Indices. *Journal of the Royal Statistical Society* (B) 41, 148–177.

GASTWIRTH, J. (1976): On Probabilistic Models of Consumer Search for Information. *Quarterly Journal of Economics* 90, 38–50.

GOTZ, G.A./MCCALL, J.J. (1984): *A Dynamic Retention Model of Air Force Officers.* RAND Corp.Rep. R-3028-AF.

GRANDMONT, J.M. (1977): Temporary General Equilibrium Theory. *Econometrica* 45, 535–572.

GRANDMONT, J.M./HILDENBRAND, W. (1974): Stochastic Processes of Temporary Equilibria. *Journal of Mathematical Economics* 1, 247–277.

GREENWOOD, H.J. (1975): Research on Internal Migration in the United States: A Survey. *Journal of Economic Literature* 13, 397–433.

HASTINGS, A./PEACOCK, J. (1975): *Statistical Distributions*, A Handbook for Students and Practitioners, Wiley, New York.

HÖNEKOPP, E. (ED.) , (1987): *Aspekte der Ausländerbeschäftigung in der BRD.* Beiträge zur Arbeitsmarkt- u. Berufsforschung, Institut für Arbeitsmarkt- und Berufsforschung der Bundesanstalt für Arbeit, 144.

KEMP, M.C./KONDO, H. (1986): An Analysis of International Migration: The Unilateral Case. In: *Economic Theory of Optimal Population,* ed. K.F. Zimmermann, Springer-Verlag, forthcoming.

KÖNIG, P. ET AL. , (1986): *Situation der ausländischen Arbeitnehmer und ihrer Familienangehörigen in der BRD.* Der Bundesminister für Arbeit und Sozialordnung (ed.).

LIPPMAN, S.A./MCCALL, J. (1976): The Economics of Job Search. *Economic Inquiry* 14, 155–189.

LIPPMAN, S.A./MCCALL, J. (1982): The Economics of Uncertainty: Selected Topics and Probabilistic Methods. In: *Handbook of Mathematical Economics* Vol. I, Arrow, K./Intriligator, M. (eds.).

MAIER, G. (1985): Cumulative causation and selectivity in labour market oriented migration caused by imperfect information. *Regional Studies* 19, 231-241.

MANDELBAUM, A. (1986): Discrete Multi-Armed Bandits and Multi-Parameter Processes. *Probability and Related Fields* 71, 129–147.

MCCALL, J. (1970): Economics of Information and Job Search. *Quarterly Journal of Economics* 84, 113–126.

MCCALL, J./MCCALL, B. (1984): *The Economics of Information: A Sequential Model of Capital Mobility.* Discussion Paper no. 186, Series A, University of Konstanz.

MCCALL, J./MCCALL, B. (1987): A Sequential Study of Migration and Job Search. *Journal of Labour Economics* 5, 452–476.

MOLHO, J. (1986): Theories of Migration. *Scottish Journal of Political Economy* 33, 396–419.

PARTHASARATHY, K.R. (1967): *Probability Measures on Metric Spaces.* Academic Press New York.

PESSINO, C. (1988): *Sequential Migration: Theory and Evidence from Peru.* University of Chicago, mimeo.

PIORE, M. (1979): *Birds of Passage.* Cambridge University Press, New York.

ROSS, S.M. (1983): *Introduction to Stochastic Dynamic Programming.* Acad. Press New York.

ROTHSCHILD, M. (1973): Models of Market Organization with Imperfect Information. *Journal of Political Economy* 81, 1283–1308.

ROTHSCHILD, M./STIGLITZ, J. (1970): Increasing Risk I. *Journal of Economic Theory* 2, 225–243.

TODARO, M. (1969): A Model of Labour Migration and Urban Unemployment in Less Developed Countries. *American Economic Review* 59, 138–148.

VARAYIA, P./WALRAND, J./BUYKHOC, C. (1984): *Extensions of the Multi-Armed Bandit Problem.* Discussion Paper, University of California at Berkeley.

WHITTLE, P. (1980): Multi–Armed Bandits and the Gittins–Index. *Journal of the Royal Statistical Society* (B) 42, 143–149.